D0857153

THE LANGUAGE OF LITERATURE

THE LANGUAGE OF LITERATURE

by

BASIL COTTLE

St. Martin's Press   New York

ISBN 0–312–46871–7

Library of Congress Cataloging in Publication Data
Cottle, Basil.
   The language of literature.
   Includes index.
   1. English language—Grammar, Historical.   2. English
literature—History and criticism.   3. English language—
Style.   4. Style, Literary. I Title.
PE1101.C67   1985   425'.09   85–2100
ISBN 0–312–46871–7

Contents

In Memoriam
Islwyn Davey Scourfield R.A.F.
† 16 June 1941

Acknowledgements

The author and publishers wish to thank the following who have kindly given permission for the use of copyright material:

Edward Arnold (Publishers) Ltd and Alfred Knopf Inc. for extract from *The Longest Journey* by E M Forster.

The Bodley Head Ltd and Random House Inc. for extract from *Ulysses* by James Joyce. Reprinted by permission of the Bodley Head Ltd and Random House Inc. from *Ulysses* by James Joyce.

Curtis Brown Group Limited and Little, Brown and Company on behalf of Ogden Nash for an extract from *Tableau at Twilight* in *Versus* (J M Dent 1949). © Ogden Nash 1949. Reproduced by permission of Curtis Brown Ltd London and Little, Brown and Company, Boston, Massachusetts.

Faber and Faber Limited for an extract from *In Parenthesis* by David Jones.

Faber and Faber Limited and Farrar, Strauss & Giroux, Inc. for an extract from Essay on Milton from *On Poetry and Poets* by T S Eliot.

David Higham Associates Limited on behalf of Dylan Thomas for an extract from *The Outing* by Dylan Thomas (Dent).

The Society of Authors as the literary representative of the Estate of A E Housman, and Jonathan Cape Ltd, publishers of A E Housman's *Collected Poems*, and Holt Rinehart & Winston on behalf of A E Housman for an extract from *A Shropshire Lad* by A E Housman.

Every effort has been made to trace all the copyright holders but if any have been inadvertently overlooked the publishers will be pleased to make the necessary arrangements at the first opportunity.

The author wishes to thank Jan Tarling for typing the manuscript.

1   The Nature of English Grammar, and its First Records

This book is written in the passionate belief that English grammar
matters, and in the serene confidence that it is pretty easy. I shall try
to exhibit the faded but real 'inflexional' system of English to a
generation that is largely ignorant of its definitions though, for the
most part, intuitively aware of its application. Our inflexional system
is that inherited method by which we add a letter, or letters, to the end
of a word (-s will spring to mind at once, and -ed and -en, and then the
elaborate -ing) to modify its function – to make a noun possess, to
make an adjective more so or most so, to make a verb past instead of
present, to turn an adjective into an adverb by adding -ly. At once, I
must add that terminations of this kind are merely the most obvious
form of inflexion; but another method is the changing of the vowel of
an irregular verb or noun – the kind of change seen in *I drink, I drank, I
have drunk* and *foot, feet* –, and Welsh changes the beginnings of words
as well.

If you have never thought about this subject before, if your
(perhaps wholly correct and handsome) handling of the language is
instinctive, I wonder what your reaction will be when I say that we
have lost most of the inflexions which we were once obliged to use, and
that we now mediate our ideas chiefly by little connectives (prepositions like *of*, *to*, *with*; snappy verbs like *do*, *did*, empty of individual
meaning)? Do you rejoice because there are fewer rules to learn,
because operative words are modified from without rather than from
within, that a sentence moves by its hidden joints rather than by its
surface flesh? That is certainly one way to look at things, but how far
would you wish to take this process of simplification, this stripping-

1

down to the basic word? Is 'me Tarzan, you Jane' the kind of English you want, and would *boy-boy* be a satisfactory version of *boys*? – it could signalise the final breakdown into an analytical language. Further, would we lose or gain in euphony and ease of speech? – 'O yonge, fresshe folkes, he or she', says Chaucer in *Troilus and Criseyde* (V. 1835), and this has ten syllables: the *-e* of *yonge* and *fresshe* is sounded, and has force, since it shows plural adjectives qualifying *folkes* (with the *-es* clearly sounded, as was the custom). The line has a regular and pretty lilt, tee-túm-tee-túm-tee-túm-tee-túm-tee-túm; *we* must give our equivalent seven syllables, 'O young, fresh folks, he or she', a broken-backed line with the monosyllables bumping into each other. But we save three syllables! – and lose no meaning! True; but are clotted consonants like *ngfr shf xh* easier to pronounce than the smaller groups in Chaucer, which have breathing-spaces between them afforded by those doomed vowels?

At the outset, we shall have to look briefly at a little Old English from the remarkable store of our pre-Conquest language, to observe the inflexional riches – or superfluous fat – that we have lost. My approach is a commonsense one; I have no *-istic* axe to grind, being in no respect a Leavisite or Structuralist or Feminist or Marxist or Linguist with a capital *L*. I hold that a misplaced 'only' *does* matter, and alters the sense, but that a split infinitive really *doesn't*. I may write in a speaking voice; this is not to popularise my material falsely, but in the belief that we should ideally write as we speak and speak as we write, possessing one language not two, and speaking to responsible and deserving persons in the same style that we would use when writing an interesting or cheering or loving or informative or persuasive letter to them.

Some matters of present-day grammar have bcome urgent; for instance, the plural of the English noun is slowly being swankified into *'s* instead of *s*: shop windows are full of CARROT'S and PARSNIP'S, a piece of ignorance that must be opposed and ended. It is 'wrong' because it is contrary to custom; in fact, it is no wronger than all the possessives singular in *'s* on nouns, only *some* of which go back to those Old English 'strong' masculine and neuter nouns that had a genitive singular in *-es*. Thus 'ship's carpenter' derives from Old English *scipes*, and the ' could be said to commemorate the lost *e*; but 'stone's-throw' derives from *stanes*, so since the derivative keeps the *e* what is the point of the apostrophe? No 'weak' nouns (their characteristic mark is a plural in *-n*), and no nouns of feminine gender, in Old English, had a genitive singular in *-es*, so the *'s* genitive is 'wrong' here every time in hundreds of nouns; the 'sun's rays' ascribes to a 'weak' feminine noun a characteristic which it never showed in its origins. Now, further to this genitive or possessive singular in an *'s* that sometimes goes back to *-es*, what of 99.99% of our plural nouns, to which we give the ending *-s*? The form with *-s* is based on the Old English 'strong' masculine plural noun in *-as*, which became *-es* in Middle English and so *-es* or *-s* in Modern English; it is historically groundless for all 'weak' nouns and all feminine and neuter nouns, and for various splinter-groups of masculines. Even if we accept it, as a sign of the force of analogy, we may suddenly wonder why it isn't spelt *'s*; as Middle English *the boyes hand* (genitive singular) now turns up as *the boy's hand*, why should not Middle English *the boyes singen* now be *the boy's sing*?

There is another official blunder yet about *-s* – the spoof form of the genitive plural. By the end of the Middle Ages it was simply the plural *boyes*, merging into *boys*; it was eventually pretended, however, that it was a special inflexion on its own, and was given the spelling, idiotic on all grounds, *-s'*. In this final position, ' replaces nothing at all; it doesn't change the pronunciation; and it suggests that we have three inflected forms of *boy* when we have only one: *boy's, boys, boys'* all sound the same, and add to the hisses and (as here) buzzes which bedevil our language. So when you see EGG'S FROM FREE-RANGE HEN'S, wince, but reflect that most *-s/-z* noises on nouns are 'wrong', anyway.

This is a sombre start to our examination of English inflexions; the commonest proves to be the product of error, analogy, and improvisation (French is no more laudable, since it has no genitive of nouns and it doesn't sound the plural *-s* except before a vowel). I am about to show from a piece of pre-Conquest verse the dependence of Old English on inflexions rather than little connectives; before which, reflect that a typical Old English 'strong' verb (the kind that changes its stem vowel in the past) or 'weak' verb (the kind that adds a dental consonant instead) will have over a dozen different inflexions expressing even more functions, whereas our worst – that is, least expressive – verbs will have three (*cut, cuts, cutting*), and the richest, even if we count in the Biblical and liturgical second person singular, will have seven, like *bind, bindest, binds, bound, boundest, binding*, and the 'extra' past participle *bounden*. Exceptional is the highly irregular *be*, with eleven (*be, am, art, is, are, was, wast* and *wert, were, being, been*). To show in action the former richness – a desperate poverty compared with the paradigms of Classical Greek – I shall reproduce the inflexions of Old English and some Middle English in **bold** type, which will always stand here for a *variety* (not a mere spelling) of inflexion which we no longer use. In these texts, I shall unwillingly use for the two single letters each representing *th*, and the one that stood in Middle English for the spirant *gh* now ascribed to the Scots on bright moonlit nights, the modern forms *th* and *gh*; they spoil the authenticity of these ancient texts, but they do not affect our theme.

The unschooled CÆDMON (elderly in 670) shyly slipped out of the feast at Whitby monastery when he saw the harp coming his way, but as he sat in the cattle-stalls an angel commanded him to sing of Creation, and he forthwith burst into:

Nu we scul**an** heri**an** heofonrices Weard,
Now we must praise heaven-kingdom's Guardian,
Metodes miht**e** and his mod**ge**thonc,
Creator's might and his heart-thought,
weorc Wuldorfæder; swa he wund**ra** gehwæs,
work Glory-father's; even as he of wonders of each,
ece Dryhten, ord onsteald**e**.
eternal Lord, beginning established.
He ærest **ge**sceop eort**han** bearn**um**,
He first shaped earth for children,
heofon to hrof**e**, halig Scypp**end**;
heaven as roof, holy shaping (one; = Creator);
tha middangeard, monncynnes Weard,
then middle-earth, mankind's Guardian,
ece Dryhten, æfter teod**e**
eternal Lord, afterwards formed
fir**um** fold**an**, Frea Ælmihtig.
for men earth, Master Almighty.

(Bede, *Historia Ecclesiastica Gentis Anglorum*, IV.24, edited by H. Sweet in *An Anglo-Saxon Reader*, Oxford, 1876, p. 47)

First, a less halting translation: 'Now we must praise heaven-kingdom's Guardian, the Creator's might, and the thought of his heart, the Glory-father's work; even as he, the eternal Lord, established the beginning of each of wonders. He first shaped the earth for his children, and heaven as a roof, the holy Creator; then mankind's Guardian, the eternal Lord, the Almighty Master, afterwards formed middle-earth, the earth for men'.

Secondly, there are three types of inflexion which we retain: the possessive singular in *heaven-kingdom's*, *Creator's*, *of each*, *mankind's*, all using -*s*; the superlative form *ærest*, 'most ere, earliest'; and the adjectival ending -*ig* on *halig*, *Ælmihtig*, now changed to -*y*. And there are ten types that we have lost; we must examine them carefully, since their ruin well demonstrates the fundamental change in attitude to inflexions, though there will be no time for this kind of thoroughness (and of course less need) as the language evolves.

Among nouns, *eorthan* and *foldan* are accusatives singular (the objects of transitive verbs) of the 'weak' feminine nouns *eorthe* and *folde*; *mihte* is the accusative singular of the 'strong' feminine noun *miht*; *hrofe* is the dative singular (the 'to/for/as' case) of the 'strong' masculine noun *hrof*, and *bearnum* and *firum* are datives plural of a 'strong' neuter and a 'strong' masculine noun; *wundra* is the genitive, possessive, but here really partitive, plural of the neuter noun *wundor*. In *modgethonc*, as in the past tense of the verb *gesceop*, we have that *ge*- which still haunts *handiwork* as an *i*, and allows the facetious archaism *yclept* 'called'. The verb forms are comparatively easy here; *herian* is an infinitive, the mark of which was -*an* and still -*en* even into the fifteenth century; *sculan* is the present indicative plural (normally *sculon*); *onstealde* and *teode* are the past tense singular of weak verbs, where we can still have the -*d* but not the -*e*; and *Scyppend* is a present participle now changed to -*ing*.

One last consideration about the inflexions of this passage which relate the words to one another: is any of them a real loss? Since we retain the pronoun *we* in saying *we shall*, would it be any more expressive for us to say *we shulan*? – especially as this -*an* stands also for the infinitive (*herian*) and the feminine noun in the accusative singular (*eorthan*, *foldan*). Feminine noun, indeed! – was grammatical gender any conceivable loss when it faded out in the fourteenth century? French and German apologists can say that it gives 'texture' to their languages, and an old Welsh lady the other day was quite indignant at the idea that nouns shouldn't go on being *hwn* and *hon* (masculine and feminine for *this*), but for no better reason than that they had always been so; and a very good reason, too – once you erode the structure of a language, it drifts towards pidgin.

Could we still do with dative nouns? There is plenty of evidence that we hanker after them, and even pretend to have them. In this passage, by using a slightly duller verb, we can still say *He made his children the earth*, as if *children* were dative (*for* them), though it bears no distinguishing mark; this would be a very poor sentence, anyway, since it could logically mean *He turned his children into the earth*, but this kind of thing happens once you slough your inflexions and then carry on as if you still had their services. And *that*, of course, is the nature of the loss we have sustained, that we are almost uninflected and we pretend that very little has happened. Well, that past tenses of 'weak' verbs have lost -*de* but just kept the -*d* matters very little, that our word *roof* hasn't a dative singular *roofe* (which would anyway have developed a silent -*e*) matters even less; but observe one casualty that is still causing muddle – the loss of the present participle in -*nd(e)*. Middle English, according to its dialect, continued to have and use present participles in -*end(e)*, -*ind(e)*, and *and(e)*; they all went down in a general ruin, and -*ing* was already the sign of the verbal noun, so two meanings began to trespass dangerously on one another. 'Do you object to me smoking?' asks the wrong question; the objection will be not to the person *me*, but to the smoking, a noun, so this noun must be possessed by the word *my*, and 'Do you object to my smoking?' is the correct form. This fusing of the verbal noun and the present participle (an adjective) is one of the most slovenly happenings in the history of English.

Cædmon lived in the second half of the seventh century; two hundred years later, the prose of KING ALFRED (849–901) will approach much nearer to our concept of 'normal', but will still be framed on an inflexional system of great complexity yet of remarkable clarity. Here he is inserting into his translation of Orosius's Latin the report of his own interview with the traveller Ohthere:

Ohthere sæde[1] his hlaforde[2], Ælfrede[2] cyninge[2], thæt
Ohthere said to his lord (to)Alfred (to)King that
he ealra[3] Northmonna[4] northmest bude[1]. He cwæth
he of all (of)Northmen northmost lived. He quoth
thæt he bude[1] on thæm[5] lande[6] northweardum[7] with
that he lived on the land northward along
tha[8] Westsæ. He sdæde[1] theah thæt thæt land
the West-Sea. He said, though, that the land
sie[9] swithe[10] lang north thonan; ac hit is
is very long north thence; but it is

eall weste[11], buton on feawum[12] stowum[13] styccemælum[12]
all waste, except in a few places piecemeal
wiciath[14] Finnas, on huntothe[2] on wintra[15], ond on
live Finns, on hunting in winter, and in
sumera[15] on fiscathe[2] be thære[16] sæ. He sæde[1]
summer on fishing by the sea. He said
thæt he æt sumum[17] cirre[2] wolde[1] fandian[18] hu longe[10]
that he at some time would test how far
thæt land northryhte[10] læge[19], oththe hwæther ænig
the land due north lay, or whether any
monn be northan thæm[5] westenne[6] bude[1]. Tha for
man to north (of) the waste lived. Then went
he northryhte[10] by thæm[5] lande[6]: let him ealne[20]
he due north along the land: (he) kept to him all
weg thæt weste[11] land on thæt steorbord, ond
(the) way the waste land on the starboard, and
tha[21] widsæ on thæt bæcbord thrie dagas.
the open sea on the port, three days.

> (King Alfred, *Orosius*, the insertion edited by H. Sweet,
> *op. cit.*, pp. 17–18)

The inflexions here will be best noted schematically, with number references:

1 Past tense singular of 'weak' verb, in -d**e**.
2 Dative singular (indirect object or after preposition) of 'strong' masculine noun, in -**e**.
3 Genitive plural of adjective, in -**ra**.
4 Genitive plural of irregular masculine noun, in -**a**.
5 Dative singular (after preposition) of neuter demonstrative/article, in -**m**.
6 Dative singular (after preposition) of 'strong' neuter noun, in -**e**.
7 Dative singular (after preposition) of neuter adjective, in -**um**.
8 Accusative singular (after *with*) of feminine demonstrative/article (agreeing with feminine noun *Westsæ*), in -**a**.
9 3rd person singular present subjunctive of verb *be*, here used inaccurately for the indicative (in a simple statement), perhaps because of the uncertainty expressed by *theah*.
10 Adverb, formed by addition to adjective of -**e**.
11 Adjective bearing an organic final -**e** even in its nominative singular masculine.

12 Dative plural (after preposition) of adjective, in -**um**.

13 Dative plural (after preposition) of 'strong' feminine noun, in -**um**.

14 3rd person plural present indicative of a 'weak' verb with -*ian* infinitive, in -**iath**.

15 Dative singular of 'strong' masculine *u*-noun, in -**a**.

16 Dative singular (after preposition) of feminine demonstrative/article (agreeing with feminine noun *sæ*), in -**re**.

17 Dative singular (after preposition) of masculine adjective (agreeing with masculine noun *cierr*), in -**um**.

18 Infinitive of 'weak' verb in -**ian**.

19 3rd person singular past subjunctive of 'strong' verb (to express hypothesis or doubt), in -**e**.

20 Accusative singular of masculine adjective (agreeing with masculine noun *weg*), in -**ne**.

21 Accusative singular of feminine demonstrative/article (agreeing with feminine noun *widsæ*), in -**a** (whereas *thæt*, which we retain as *that*, is the accusative singular neuter, agreeing with the neuter nouns *steorbord*, *bacbord*).

In this passage of 108 words, 42 share 21 inflexions that we no longer want (whether we *need* some of them is another matter); 14 words are in an inflexional system to which we still adhere – *he* (seven times), *him*, *his*, *hit* (our *it*), *northmest* (our -*most*), *ænig* (our -*y*), and *Finnas* and *dagas* (which will slide through -*es* to *Finns* and *days*). So 56 words are inflected! Do you find this excessive? – and on the other hand do you shrink from a pidgin language that calls a piano 'big black box, you hit him, he cry'? There *is* a happy mean between these, and it would be lovely to think that it is the present grammar of our matured language.

If we continued with this passage of Alfred for twice as long again, new glories or lumber would emerge. Various inhabitants appear – hwælhunt**an**, hunt**an**, fisceras, fugeleras; the two last are our familiar *fishers* and *fowlers*, but the other two are 'weak' masculine plural nouns in -**an**, *whalehunters* and *hunters*. Ohthere begins to speak of his exploring-party in the plural, the past tense of which is in -**on**, so they cird**on** (*turned*) and dorst**on** (*durst*, *dared*), and there wær**on** (*were*) Finns, and the Permians hafd**on** (*had*) their land well tilled. One other form (not properly an inflexional feature) must suffice from this passage: Ohthere wisse (*knew*) one thing about the topography, but nysse (*didn't know*) various other things. We have almost lost the negative verb, but it clings on in *willy-nilly*, a magnificent relic of three-fold archaism: (1) if you reverse the order of pronoun-subject and verb, you form an *if*-clause ('Had I known –'), so here *will I* = 'if I will'; (2) *will* in Middle English means not a future but a wish or intention, so here *will I* in fact means 'if I want to'; (3) Middle English *ne will I* turned into *nill I* 'if I don't want to'. So *willy-nilly* is an epitome of older uses, and I hope that my readers will retain it and perpetuate it.

We must leave Old English. Readers with antiquarian tastes will be feeling wistful, whereas blunt, pragmatic speakers will be left quite wistless. It has not been practical or reasonable to present the full panoply of inflexions, though a number of those not mentioned will occur when we pass on now to Middle English, and some are still astonishingly with us, hiding in mis-spellings and misconceptions – as we shall see later in a less densely textual period of refreshment. But at least we, with nothing to remember about nouns save sticking an *s* on (and dear old *oxen* and *children*, with a couple of similar archaisms, and *mice* and *lice* and *men's feet*, and some *sheep* and *deer* and *swine*), can gasp with more relief than disgust at having lost three grammatical genders, four cases (to which the instrumental is sometimes added), various types of declension (as in Latin), and the distinguishing marks of all the plurals. I have been referring throughout to 'strong' and 'weak' nouns, too; the difference between them is of academic interest, and the terms 'strong' and 'weak' are all the less satisfactory in that they bear no useful relation to 'strong' and 'weak' verbs and adjectives, but these nouns *are* utterly different from each other, and the 'weak' ones could easily have prevailed and *oxen* become the norm instead of the freak. We should then have had a much prettier language, but the Normans, in evil day, had -*s* plurals in their language, too, and the scales were tipped. Long live oxen!

We have thrown out all inflexions of adjectives, save for the comparative and superlative -*er* and -*est*. This was a shrewd move, save that it came by chance, not choice; inflected adjectives, with their three genders, two numbers, five cases (the extra one being the instrumental), and their 'weak' and 'strong' forms, really contributed nothing at all to expressiveness, and we are to be congratulated that their eleven feasible shapes have been reduced to one. The numerals had their own genders and cases, and though we have found it necessary to retain the elaborate pronoun system (our *I*, *me*, *mine*, *me* is as full as in Old English), we have not included in this the provision of 'duals', whereby Old English didn't have to spell out *we two*, *us two*, *of us two*, and *to us two*, but just had *wit*, *unc*, *uncer*, *unc*, with *git*, *inc*, *incer*, *inc* for the 2nd person.

Of Old English verbs we have lost very much of the internal inflexional system, but retained the framework – the 'classes' of verbs; once again, we use those flaccid terms 'weak' for the verbs that add *-d/-t* and 'strong' for those that change their stem vowel. The excellent list of over 250 irregular verbs given in the Longman *Dictionary of Contemporary English* (1978), pp. 1289–92, includes compounds like *forget* as well as *get*, and a number of irregular 'weak' verbs like *catch–caught* and *make–made*, but the remainder are an impressive list of old 'strong' forms defying time and lasting on as *spring–sprang–sprung* and the like. Analogy is always undermining them, and rarish verbs like *thrive–throve–thriven* may nearly have reached the end of their days, but we are apparently fond of them, and make up joky 'strong' forms like 'I grun at him' (from *grin*) or irregular 'weak' ones like 'The Vicar praught' (from *preach*, on the basis of *teach*). But we are perhaps worrying overmuch about mere endings and their proliferation; a loss that *does* matter lies in our neglect of expressive parts of verbs, which are still available but are dying of attrition. I certainly do not mean that diseased old member the gerund, or 'dative infinitive', or 'dative of the verbal noun', which abjectly depended on a preceding *to*; an infinitive like *ridan* 'to ride' and its gerund 'to ridenne' had the same function, but the gerund limped on, in the case of a few short verbs and still ending *-ne*, until Chaucer's time. This was no loss, but the slow atrophy of the subjunctive mood of verbs has entailed a real loss of subtlety.

2 Middle English Grammar: Verse

By 1066, and for 150 years afterwards, English was in a disappointing state, to judge by what little has survived. This fact of survival must always be borne in mind; *Sir Gawain and the Green Knight*, a masterpiece of fourteenth-century English, survives in one scruffily-written man-uscript where the right-hand pages are sometimes folded back with indecent haste on to the left-hand ones, thereby blotting them, and the pictures are like pavement-art, but without it we should be ignorant of one of the peaks of our mediaeval culture. Yet the signs are that the Old English poetic idiom *was* wearing out, admitting Frenchified rhyme to the detriment of the native alliteration, and allowing its line to bloat. The language was carried along with this slack tide; no magnates commissioned it (they wanted Norman French), the 'occupying power' spoke Norman French, features of Norman French grammar affected English (especially, as we have seen, in the vogue for -*s* plurals on nouns), and features of Norman French syntax affected the syntax in such ways as the use of (what are now) *de* and *à* for our declined genitive and dative of nouns.

Some of the wrenchings of the language were disastrous. But the imposition or peaceful acquisition of so many 'Romance' words (from Latin *via* Norman French, and later *via* the French of Paris) has been an enrichment, giving us the biggest vocabulary of any language; this is not properly part of our theme, but as almost all the new words were pressed into the language as regular 'strong' nouns and 'weak' verbs, their effect on flattening out the inflexions was very brutal. Since there is little up to about 1200 which is worth reading as literature, I think it may be best to introduce Middle English not chronologically but by exhibiting some of its lost characteristics (along with those that we have inherited) in a series of short extracts from various periods and hands and on different subjects. To illustrate the subjunctive, to

11

which just now I ascribed a degree of subtlety, I have chosen a miracle of the Holy Cross, from the *South English Legendary*, composed possibly at Gloucester round about 1300:

A nonne[1] ther was in an abbey that a dai yeode[2]
A nun there was in an abbey who one day went
  pleie.[3]
  to enjoy herself.
An erbe[4] that me clupeth[14] letuse[4] heo fond bi the weie[5].
A plant that one calls lettuce she found by the path.
Ther of heo nom and et a lef, and ne blessede[2] it
Of it she took and ate a leaf, and blessed it not
  noght er.
  at all first.
Anon heo bicom out of witte[5] and fel adoun right ther.
At once she went out of her wits and fell down right there.
Gret deol made that folk for hure, and echman that
Great grief made the people for her, and everyone who
  hure say.
  her saw.
An holyman that ther of hurde[2] thuderward wende[2]
A holy man who of it heard thither went
  a day.
  one day.
Anon so he com touward hure, the devel gradde[2]
As soon as he came towards her, the devil screamed
  for fere[5],
  for fear,
'A weilawei! Wat dude[2] ich here bote sat up an
'Oh, alack! What did I here save sit upon a
  erbe[4] there?
  plant there?
And heo nom me and swolwe me in, and bot me wel
And she took me and swallowed me in, and bit me very
  sore[6].
  sorely.
Thou might me wite[3] wat thou wolt, ac i nabbe[7]
Thou canst blame me what thou wantest, but I haven't
  gult namore'.
  guilt any further'.

'Thou sselt', quath this holyman, 'another in habb**e**[3]
'Thou shalt', said this holy man, 'another lodging
    to yer**e**[8].
    have two years.
For heo foryet to bless**e**[3] hure, wel **i**redi[15]
Because she forgot to bless herself, very prompt
    thou were'.
    thou wert'.
Thoru sign**e**[3] of the holi crois the devel he drof
Through sign of the Holy Cross the devil he drove
    out there.
    out there.
Yolling**e**[9] he flei awei with wel grislich ber**e**[5].
Yelling he flew away with very horrible clamour.
                     [*not* 'a grizzly bear']
Therefore ich red**e**[7] ech mon **beo**[16] war, that
Therefore I advise each man beware, who
    wiln**eth**[14] wel to do:
    wants well to do:
Bless**i**[17] is mete[10] ar he it ete[11], that he ne **beo**[16]
Let him bless his food ere he it eat, that he not be
    served so.
    served so.
Now, God, for the rode[12] love[5] that thou were on **i**do,[15]
Now, God, for the cross's love that Thou wert on putt,
Bring us to the heie[13] joie[4] that thou us boght**est**[18] to.
Bring us to the high joy that Thou boughtest us for.
                  [or 'boughtest for us'].

I have not reproduced in **bold** all the inflexions or the parts of pronouns; spelling of English at this time was unstandardised, fragmented into dialects, not taught, and innocent of any dictionary. Of the 36 (the majority) that I have left, you should notice at once that 29 are simply -**e**. This is sinister – what happens when most inflexions are just -**e**, especially when this final letter is very vulnerable to a following vowel? When the devil first screams, it is clear that he gabbles 'Wat dud' ich here'; the holy man uses the 'sign' of the 'holi crois', and because elision of -e also takes place before an unstressed *h-*, we obviously have to say 'Yolling' he flei'. The operative final -**e** became less and less of a reality: the maid-of-all-work among the inflexions became unable to isolate the various meanings which it had inherited from the decrepit post-Conquest system. When I wrote *The Triumph of English: 1350–1400* (London: Blandford Press, 1969) a reviewer was very scornful because, after I had listed the twenty-odd functions of final *-e* in the various parts of speech, I referred to the 'paradoxical situation . . . whereby *-e* . . . defined almost everything and therefore satisfactorily defined almost nothing'. This remains an accurate statement; perhaps she had found my colloquial remark that *-e* 'stood (though it sometimes fell) for' various parts a little flippant. Anyway, by the death of Chaucer in 1400 *-e* was moribund, though it had greatly enriched his music and would still be *written* and (by poetasters, when they needed it for a syllable) sounded.

Yet here the era is the beginning of the fourteenth century, and *-e* is still vigorous. Let us extricate its functions in this story of the nun:

1 Final vowel of the Old English 'weak' feminine noun *nunne*.
2 3rd person singular past tense of 'weak' verb.
3 Infinitive of verb, a broken-down form of Old English *-an* and then Middle English *-en*.
4 Original final *-e* on an imported French noun.
5 Dative singular (after preposition) of noun.
6 Adverb adding *-e* to adjective *sor* (from Old English *sar*).
7 1st person singular present tense of verb (negative).
8 Probably a version of the Old English uninflected plural *gear* 'years'.
9 The first replacement for the early Middle English present participle *-ende/-inde* in the Midlands and South was *-inge*, later becoming *-ing*.
10 Organic final vowel of Old English noun *mete*.
11 3rd person singular present subjunctive.
12 Genitive singular ('of the cross') of 'strong' feminine noun.
13 Adjective in 'weak' position after definite article.

However much one may regret the passing of the pretty lilt which *-e* gave to Middle English, this state of affairs is ridiculous: thirteen hinges, nuances, and positive changes in meaning, conveyed by the same little murmur, so weak that it slurred into a following vowel. The other inflexions, which I have numbered subsequently to these, are sturdier:

14 3rd person singular present indicative, as still found in the King James Bible and the Book of Common Prayer.

15 **i-** from Old English prefix *ge-*.

16 3rd person singular present subjunctive of *be* (West Midland dialect).

17 Form of the 3rd person singular present subjunctive of a 'weak' *-ian* verb (*bletsian* in Old English).

18 2nd person singular past tense of 'weak' verb, as surviving (like 14) in the traditional usage of the Church of England.

I promised to use this passage to commend the status of the subjunctive. Here we have four examples of this 'mood' in two adjacent lines: 'I advise every man *be* ware', 'Let him bless' all in one word, 'before he *eat* it', and 'so that he *be* not treated like that'. These are variously a warning of what to do, an encouragement to a course of action not always adhered to, the poised moment before a hypothetical happening, and the method of avoiding a possible penalty. For these hypotheses, the tentative subjunctive is used, where we would have an infinitive *to be*, the curiously ugly *let him bless* as if someone has to permit him, the indicative *eats* (this suggests he will definitely eat it) or (better) *eating*, and the blunt *isn't*. An expensive subtlety, perhaps, but one that suggests the delicacy of Middle English.

One idiom needs a note before we relinquish this story: *an erbe that me clupeth letuse* 'a plant that one calls lettuce'. This *me*, with a short vowel, has nothing to do with our *mē*; it is a progressive reduction of *man* to *men* and so, with the *-n* lost as in so many other forms, *me*, the equivalent of French *on* and German *Man* and Modern English *one*. Yet we find 'It gives one spots before one's eyes' rather too genteel, and the real equivalent is a passive verb, 'a plant which is called lettuce'.

It would obviously help the reader of this Middle English material to know how it sounded. The subject is a large one, and not conclusively worked out, but a reasonable guide to it (and especially to the sounds of Chaucer) is in my *Triumph of English*, pp. 33*ff*. As a general rule, every consonant should be pronounced, since scribes wrote what they heard (not what they looked up in non-existent dictionaries), and *world* must have sounded much more like *worruld* than like the 'dark' consonants and the *uh* of the present word. Final *-e* should be sounded, except (as we have seen) before a vowel or an unstressed *h-*. Most difficult of all, the long vowels $\bar{a}, \bar{e}, \bar{\imath}/\bar{y}, \bar{o}, \bar{u}$ should be kept pure, with two forms of both $\bar{e}$ and $\bar{o}$, as in *father, bay* and *bear, machine, go* and *boar*, and *zoo*, with an extra French *u* and German *ü* vowel in the South and West, spelt *u*, and in the same area the French *oeuf* and German *Börse* vowel, spelt bewilderedly as *oe, eo, ue, eu, o, u,* even *uu*. The short vowels are enough like ours, provided we imitate *pat, pet, pit, pot* and *put* (not *cut*). The diphthongs presumably sounded like their two dismembered vowels put together again.

Since I have regretted the near death of the subjunctive, I shall now go back one hundred years to the Worcestershire epic poet LAGHAMON (who flourished round about 1200), to record a group of forms which contributed more complexity than rich texture, the declined number '2'. Arthur's last battle has just ended, Modred and all the other traitors have been slain, and Arthur has received a ghastly spear-wound:

> Fiftene he hafde feondliche wund**en**.
> *Fifteen he had devilish wounds.*
> Mon mihte i thare lasten **twa** glov**en** ithraste.
> *One could have in their least two gloves thrust.*
> Tha nas ther na mare i than feht**e** to lav**e**,
> *Then was not there no more in the fight as a remnant,*
> Of **twa** hundred thusend monn**en** tha ther leien
> *Of two hundred thousand men who there lay*
>   tohauwen,
>   *hewn to bits,*
> Buten Arthur the king ane and of his cnihtes
> *Save Arthur the king only and of his knights*
>   **tweien.**
>   *two.*

>   (Laghamon, *Brut*, edited by G. L. Brook and R. F. Leslie,
> Early English Text Society, 1978, II. 748, ll. 14, 261–14, 265)

Laghamon retains the three forms of '2' according to gender: *twa*, the feminine form, with the feminine plural noun 'gloves'; *twa*, also the neuter form, with the neuter noun 'hundred'; *tweien* (our *twain*), the masculine form, with the masculine noun 'knights'.

At first, then, this passage looks very conservative and correct; but *wunden* and *gloven* are really from feminine 'strong' nouns, and Laghamon has given them 'weak' *-en* plurals (there is admittedly a rare 'weak' version *glofe*). The inflexion of *monnen* is an evolved form of Old English *-um*, the dative plural of nouns. The *-e* on *fehte* and *lave* is dative after the prepositions *in* and *to*. The double negative 'there was not no more' doesn't cancel out in Middle English, but emphasises. And 'in their least' must now have partitive, not possessive, expression – 'in the least/smallest of them'.

In the same era, *ca.* 1200, the presumed poet of *The Owl and the Nightingale*, NICHOLAS OF GUILDFORD, Vicar of Portesham in Dorset, was using a healthily simplified declension of nouns and adjectives, a fairly conservative verb system, and that very old-fashioned version of the '2' idiom, the dual pronoun. His two contestants have agreed on nothing save the worth, the impartiality, and the brilliance of Nicholas of Guildford, to whose arbitration they are about to submit their long dispute:

'Certes', cwath the Hule, 'that is soth.
'Indeed', said the Owl, 'that is true.
Theos riche men wel muche misdoth
These rich men very much misdo
That leteth thane gode mon
When they abandon the good man
That of so feole thinge con,
Who of so many things knows,
And yiveth rente wel misliche,
And give income very amiss,
And of him leteth wel lihtliche.
And esteem him very casually.
With heore cunne heo beoth mildre,
With their kindred they are kinder,
An yeveth rente litle childre:
And give income to little children:
Swa heore wit hi demth a dwole,
So their sense them judges in error,
That ever abid Maistre Nichole.
In that always waits Master Nicholas.
Ah ute we thah to him fare,
But let us though to him go,

For thar is unker dom all yare'.
For there is of us two the judgment all ready'.
'Do we', the Nightegale seide;
'Let's do that', the Nightingale said;
'Ah wa schal unker speche rede,
'But who shall of us two the speech declare,
An telle tovore unker deme?'
And speak before of us two the judge?'
'Tharof ich schal the wel icweme',
'In that I shall thee well satisfy',
Cwath the Houle, 'for al, ende of orde,
Said the Owl, 'for all, to end from beginning,
Telle ich con, word after worde'.
Speak I can, word after word'.

Three times he uses the 1st person dual genitive *unker*, and the duals will not long survive his time; a number of languages have had duals for things that normally come in pairs, like hands and ears and eyes, but in any other case the argument against them is 'if duals, why not trinals? – or shorthand words for sets of four?' In other respects, Nicholas – a witty and sophisticated writer – shows a much more 'modern' language than his contemporary Laghamon. Yet there are still strong dialect features which mark his language off from what will become standard use: the 3rd person plural present indicative in the South-West ended in *-th* (we still have it in the Winchester College motto 'Manners makyth man'), so here occur *misdoth*, *leteth* (twice), *yiveth*, *beoth*, *yeveth*. One of the most archaic phrases is *thane gode man*: *-ne* shows the masculine accusative singular of the article, and *gode* has an *-e* because it is an adjective in the 'weak' position after an article. Some datives survive – *with* governs *cunne*, and in the last two lines 'to end' and 'from beginning' are marked by a simple dative and a dative governed by *from*, with the accusative *word* in the next line and the dative *worde* governed by *after*. But, extremely early by comparison with many later texts, the infinitive has lost its *-n* – *fare*, *rede*, *telle*, *icweme*, *Telle*.

Just as Laghamon epitomised the three genders of '2' in four lines, so in *Saint Erkenwald*, written by an unknown? Cheshire writer in the late 1300s, there is a convenient two-line baptismal formula which presents three forms of the genitive singular noun; the metre is alliterative.

> I folwe the in the Fader nome and his fre Childes
> And of the gracious Holy Goste ('I baptise thee in the Name of the
> Father and his noble Child and the gracious Holy Spirit').

It would be inconceivable now for us to mix these three forms – *Fader* (nouns of relationship were not inflected in the singular, which also accounts for *mother-tongue*, 'language of the mother'), *Childes* (retaining the genitive singular inflexion in full), and *of the Holy Goste* (the expanded 'analytical' form using *of*). The second two methods remain, though the language is happier when only one method is used at a time. And of course there were other ways of forming the genitive singular: 'strong' feminine nouns in general used -*e*, and this influenced the forms without -*s* seen in *Lady Day* (the day of St Mary the Virgin, called by Roman Catholics 'Our Lady'), *Lady Chapel*, the insect *ladybird* (said to be under her patronage) and the flower *ladysmock* recalling her blue gown. All 'weak' nouns had genitives in Old English -*an* and Middle English -*en*, now camouflaged in our *Sunday* and *Monday*, the first halves of which were *sunnan* 'of the (feminine) sun' and *monan* 'of the (masculine) moon' – whereas *Tuesday*, *Wednesday* and *Thursday* are named from 'strong' male deities possessing in -*s*, *Friday* from a 'strong' goddess who has lost her internal -*e*, and *Saturday* from the pagan Latin god Saturnus.

3 Middle English Grammar: Prose

It will now be realistic to turn from verse, and from the features of a fading grammar, to a confident all-purposes prose with a modern look and the good fortune to be written in that East Midland dialect which became Standard English. 'SIR JOHN MANDEVILLE' (his name should live in inverted commas, since – like most of his book – it is itself a fiction) came out in French and was quickly translated into an English which *well* covered the requirements of its history, geography, description, speculation and devotion. For its competence, and because of its not surprising popularity, the prose of 'Mandeville' may reasonably be called the founding father of our prose, and it has had many adherents. Though the text cannot be precisely dated, it probably precedes the mature work of Chaucer and the poets of *Piers Plowman* and *Sir Gawain and the Green Knight*.

Read this passage first without consulting the Modern English version that I append; you should find most of it fairly easy, but it still requires the use of **bold** for some inflexions, and you will see that they are neither all consistent nor by any means all modern. (This is from the abridged version in Bodleian MS. E Musaeo 116, ed. M. C. Seymour, Early English Text Society, 1963, p. 13).

It is for to wet**yn**[1] that thow it be so that the Grekis are[7] Cristene men, yit they vary**en**[6] from us in manye poyntys that fallyth to oure lawe; for they sey**n**[5] that the Holy Gost comyth not from the Sone but only from the Fadyr, and they obey**e**[7] not to the Court of Rome ne to the Pape, but they sey**n**[5] and trow**yn**[5] and affermy**n**[5] that here patriark in here contre hath as meche power as oure Pape here. Johan that was Pape of Rome the XXII, he wrot his letteres and sente to hem and seyde that all Cristente shulde **be**[2] as on and

20

undyr the power of hym that were Cristis vekyr and the successour of Peter, to whom that Oure Lord yaf the power to bynde[3] and unbynde[3]; wherfore that hym thoughte that they shulde obeyse[3] to his ordenaunce of holy cherche as to the verry successour of Seynt Petyr. The Grekys wretyn ageyn to the Pape in this maner: 'Thyn sovereyn powyr aboutyn thyn subjectis we trowe[7] it stedfastly. Thyn sovereyn pryde may we nat takyn[1] away, ne thyn sovereynte of averyce wele we nat ben[4] aboute to fulfille[3]. God be with the, for he is with us'. Othir answere than thus myghte the Pape not getyn[1] of hem. The Grekys make[7] the sacrement of the auter of sour bred, and seyn[5] that we erryn[5] that makyn[5] it of bred not sour. They dreyen[6] here bred in the sonne and kepyn[5] it thourw al the yer, and therwith they hoselyn[5] here seke men.

(It is to be known that, though it is so that the Greeks are Christian men, yet they vary from us in many points that belong to our law; for they say that the Holy Spirit proceeds not from the Son but only from the Father, and they do not obey the Curia of Rome or the Pope, but they say and believe and affirm that their Patriarch in their country has as much power as our Pope here. John XXII, who was Pope of Rome, wrote his letters and sent them to them and said that all Christendom should be as one and under the power of whoever was Christ's Vicar and the successor of St Peter, to whom Our Lord gave the power to bind and unbind; so it seemed to him that they should obey his ordinance of Holy Church as being the true successor of St Peter. The Greeks wrote back to the Pope in this manner: 'We steadfastly believe your supreme power over your subjects. We cannot take away your supreme pride, and we are not going to fulfil your supremacy in avarice. God be with you, because he is with us'. Other answer than that the Pope could not get from them. The Greeks make the sacrament of the altar out of leavened bread, and say that we are wrong in making it of unleavened bread. They dry their bread in the sun and keep it all through the year, and with it they housel [give the Sacrament to] their sick people).

I have numbered 1–4 the inflexions of the infinitive – three in -**yn**, one without anything, four in -**e**, one in -**en**. The number 5 emphatically marks the -**yn** inflexion of the 1st and 3rd person plural present indicative of verbs – this occurs nine times; 6 shows the use of the more familiar -**en**, and 7 mere -**e**. The phrase *poyntys that fallyth to oure lawe* is strange; *fallyth* is strictly singular in this dialect (as in *comyth* just afterwards), and this error may arise from 'attraction' to the singular noun *lawe*. The past tense shows the *-n* plural – *wretyn*; the 'weak' past tense singular is in *-e* (*sente, seyde, thoughte, myghte*), and the 'strong' is seen in *wrot*, uninflected.

The subjunctive occurs after 'though' at the beginning, in the wish *God be with the*, and with great force, in its past tense, in *hym that were Cristis vekyr* – meaning him who at any time or in any circumstances might ever be Christ's Vicar. In *Sir Gawain and the Green Knight*, l.85, we are told that 'Arthure wolde not ete til al were served'; *al* is singular, and so is the past subjunctive *were* ('If I were you'), so the meaning is not that he waited until everyone had been served, and then fell to, but that he intended ('willed') not to eat until everyone conceivable should have been served.

It is probable that *manye* and *seke* are true plural adjectives in *-e*. The paradigm of the 3rd person plural pronoun is clearly *they, hem, here, hem*, a series familiar in the near-contemporary East-Midlander Chaucer. Altogether, we feel fairly at ease with this passage, and the many inflexions in *-n* also keep it tuneful and flowing; inflexions in *-s*, on the other hand, are not at all obtrusive, and the inflexional vowel with them can't make its mind up between *i, y* and *e*, in *Grekis, poyntys, letteres*. Mere *-e* is on the way out, and when it *does* occur after Chaucer one almost gets the impression (though quite wrongly, I hope) that the writer is using it to make his text look olde, as in *Ye Olde Tea-Shoppe* (where *Y* is a misshaping of 'thorn' = *th*); the impression that a poet is using *-e* to get an extra syllable may often be more accurate.

The language had by the end of the fourteenth century reached a much more promising stage in its career. Grammatical gender had faded out; the declined adjective had *-e* or nothing (and even the *-e* would soon be extinct, and mourned by none); the typical noun (based on the 'strong' masculine) had its quiverful of *s*s, and – decreasingly – a dative singular in *-e*, while the less familiar 'weak' noun with *-n* plural was capitulating everywhere, though the *oxen* have beefed their way through to our century; the other freaks, of the *man–men* and *sheep–sheep* types, have shown similar resilience. The verb system had, *according to dialect*, still preserved a number of the old subtleties, but it would be quite wrong to assume that it was more expressive than ours; its utility varied – there was advantage in having *will* to mean 'want' and *shall* to mean 'must', in expressing doubt and wish and so forth with a subjunctive, and in being able to question and deny with straightforward 'Know you?' and 'I know you not' and 'Know you not?', without the ugly little *do* (but that was a matter of syntax, the word as a neighbour, not of grammar, the word as an individual). On the other hand, the past tenses were poorly provided for: very often, the simple past was in use for our perfect ('I have gone'), pluperfect ('I had gone'), and past continuous ('I was going'). The force of analogy had worked wisely in some cases, especially in the levelling to one form of the singular and plural past tense of 'strong' verbs; so where Old English had four 'principal parts' to its 'strong' verbs – *drincan* (infinitive), *dranc* (past singular), *druncon* (past plural), *druncen* (past participle) – Middle English settled down eventually to the three which *we* know: *drink, drank* (singular and plural), *drunk(en)*, save when our associates say 'we drunk', with history on their side.

When people say 'Chaucer is one of *us*', it suggests superficial reading, though I can see what makes them say it; the vocabulary has to be mastered before we can pretend to read 'He was a verray, parfit, gentil knyght', since *very, perfect* and *gentle* do not now mean what Chaucer is getting at, and a modern knight little resembles Chaucer's dignified mercenary. But when we hear lucidly of the Clerk 'And gladly wold**e** he lern**e** and gladly teche', the *-e* of the past tense singular, and of the two infinitives, does not impede us, but it's still there.

One more passage, written quite close on events of 1433 or 1434, shall receive the full 'treatment' of numbered annotation, because it shows the highly inflected language in the last throes of its existence yet by no means at war with an easy, modern style. It has merits as prose: MARGERY KEMPE, the plucky, coarse-grained, self-centred would-be mystic of King's Lynn, is always an interesting figure to study. She kept a diary, where her devotions and ecstasies predominate, but alongside rumbustious adventures, the odd obscene dream, her sharp repartee, and resourceful visits to Jerusalem, Rome, Santiago, Danzig, Aachen and (informally, by shipwreck) Norway. Her courage in keeping a diary at all is astounding – she was illiterate, and three secretaries in succession thus produced the first autobiography in English, the first extended life of a lay-person in English, the first book by a woman in English apart from Julian of Norwich, (it has 254 big printed pages in the Early English Text Society edition of 1940), and probably the longest original untranslated work in Middle

English prose. She also found time to have umpteen children, with hardly a survivor that we hear of, and to mill and brew. Her company was sometimes less stimulating; the Sacrament disturbed her, and she reacted with hysteria and screams, and in the following passage she has just been ditched in the middle of Germany by her male escort, who was sick of the embarrassment she was causing. But God commanded her that night to go to church first thing in the morning, and there she would find company:

On the next day be-tyme she payd for hir lodgynge[1], speryng at (*enquiring of*) hir oostys[2] yf thei knewe[3] of any felaschep to-Akun-ward (*bound for Aachen*). Thei seyd, 'Nay'. Sche, takyng hir leve of hem, went to the chirche[1] for to felyn[4] & prevyn[4] (*prove/test*) yf hir felyng (she now makes it a *hunch* rather than the word of God) wer[5] trewe[6] er (*or*) not. Whan sche cam ther, sche saw a cumpany of powr folke[1]. Than went sche to on of hem, speryng whidyr thei wer purposyd[7] to gon[8]. He seyd, 'To Akun'. Sche preyid[9] hym that he wolde[10] suffyr[11] hir to gon[8] in her cumpany. 'Why, dame', he seyd, 'hast thu no man to gon[8] wyth the?' 'No', sche seyde, 'my man is gon[12] fro me'. So sche was receyvyd[7] in-to a cumpany of powr folke[1], &, whan thei comyn[13] to any towne[1], she bowte[14] hir mete[15] & hir felaschep went on beggyng (*a-begging*). Whan thei wer[16] wyth-owtyn the townys[2], hir felaschep dedyn[13] of (*took off*) her clothys[2], & sittyng nakyd[7], pykyd[17] hem. Nede[18] compellyd[19] hir to abydyn[4] hem & prolongyn[4] hir jurne & ben[8] at meche[20] mor cost than sche xulde[10] ellys[21] a (*have*) ben. Thys creatur was a-bavyd (*abashed*) to putte[22] of hir clothis[23] as hyr felawys[2] dedyn[13], & therfor sche thorow hir comownyng (*keeping company*) had part of her vermyn & was betyn[24] (*bitten*) & srongyn[24] ful evyl (*very nastily*) bothe day & nyght tyl God sent hir other felaschep. Sche kept forth (*on with*) hir felaschep wyth gret angwisch & disese (*discomfort*) & meche lettyng (*delaying*) un-to the tyme that thei comyn[13] to Akun.

A table of the inflexions will look complicated, but they will not have hampered our reading:

1 Possible dative singular in -e after preposition.
2 Plural noun in -ys.
3 Past tense plural of 'strong' verb in -e.
4 Infinitive in -yn;

5 Past subjunctive singular, to express doubt.

6 Organic -**e** on adjective, from Old English *treowe*.

7 Past participle of 'weak' verb in -**yd**.

8 Infinitive in -**n**.

9 Past tense singular of 'weak' verb in -**id**.

10 Past tense singular of 'weak' verb in -**de**.

11 Infinitive without inflexion.

12 Past participle of 'strong' verb lacking the -*e* of Modern English.

13 Past tense plural of 'strong' verb in -**yn**.

14 Past tense singular of 'weak' verb in -**te**.

15 Organic -**e** on noun, from Old English *mete* (*food*).

16 Past tense plural of verb *to be* without inflexion.

17 Past tense plural of 'weak' verb in -**yd**.

18 -**e** added to 'strong' feminine noun even in nominative.

19 Past tense singular of 'weak' verb in -**yd**.

20 -**e** kept to show adverb?

21 -**ys** for Old English -*es* in *elles*.

22 Infinitive in -**e**.

23 Plural noun in -**is**.

24 Past participle of 'strong' verb in -**yn**.

The apparent richness of this display is partly due to the dissolute spelling: the infinitive has four possible endings – our own (with no inflection), -*yn*, -*n*, -*e*; -*ys* is a version of -*is*, -*yd* of *id*; *yn* serves also the past tense and the past participle; -*e* is still too busy. Syntactically, there are few difficulties, though the abrupt idiom 'she paid, . . . asking', 'She, taking her leave . . . went', 'Then went she to one of them, asking', would not now be so frequent; these three present participles are also too close to the *real* original -*ing* forms, the verbal nouns *lodgynge, felyng, beggyng, comownyng, lettyng*. There is a nice use of the subjunctive *wer* when Margery is wondering how reliable her intuition is; and *is gon* shows the continued use of the verb *to be* in conjugating an intransitive verb, where our correct form is certainly now *has gone*. She fortunately distinguishes consistently between the possessives *hir* 'her' and *her* 'their', so it is clear that these beggars took off *their* clothes and deloused them.

That passage from Mrs Kempe bristled with inflexions, some of them futile, but proved on reading to be close to our own narrative style.

The *Morte Darthur*, composed by SIR THOMAS MALORY some time before 1485, when Caxton printed it, tends and waters the outdated chivalry of the 'Roses' century; do not the less subtle historians officially date the end of the Middle Ages to the Battle of Bosworth, in the very year of its publication? The grand climactic book, on the death of the King itself, begins seductively but soon moves closer to nausea than to nostalgia, and neither can make an adequate all-purposes prose style.

In May, whan every harte floryshyth and burgenyth (for, as the season ys lusty to beholde and comfortable, so man and woman rejoysyth and gladith of somer commynge with his freyshe floures, for wynter wyth hys rowghe wyndis and blastis causyth lusty men and women to cowre and to syt by fyres), so thys season hit befelle in the moneth of May a grete angur and unhapp that stynted nat tylle the floure of chyvalry of the worlde was destroyed and slayne.

And all was longe uppon two unhappy knyghtis whych were named sir Aggravayne and sir Mordred, that were brethirn unto sir Gawayne. For thys sir Aggravayne and sir Mordred had ever a prevy hate unto the quene, dame Gwenyver, and to sir Launcelot; and dayly and nyghtly they ever wacched uppon sir Launcelot.

The most striking inflexion here will not surprise anyone familiar with the 1611 Bible or the Prayer Book – the *-yth*, *-ith* (though we normally spell it *-eth*) of the 3rd person singular present indicative; it is good old standard East Midland, our present *-s* being a parvenu from Northern and Scots, and *floryshyth*, *burgenyth*, *causyth*, *rejoysyth* and *gladith* are as expected. So what is the infinitive doing? – shall we find an exciting *-n* still clinging on? No – the forms are *beholde*, *cowre*, *syt*, just *-e* twice and a blank. There might be two plural adjectives, *freyshe* and *rowghe*, carefully given *-e* which, if meant, would be sounded before the consonants *f-* and *w-*. Plural nouns of the regular sort end in *-is* (*wyndis*, *blastis*, *knyghtis*) or *-es* (*fyres*); but the irregular *men* and *women* are unshakeable (as they still are) and the highly irregular *brethirn* has not yet given way to *brothers*. The form *brethren*, still used in liturgies and (I believe) the occult, is a mistaken extension of the 'weak' *-en* plural, and so is *children*; *oxen* is, as we have seen, the only real 'weak' plural surviving, because I have never met those old ladies you hear about who call their shoes and socks their *shoon* and *hosen*, and because *treen*, now so often used in Folk Museums on cases containing wooden objects, is not really a noun at all but an adjective, Old English *treowen*, 'made of wood'. So remember, try to mention oxen every day, that they perish not.

Otherwise, the difficulties here are semantic and not our concern; but for completeness observe that *lusty* is 'jolly' (full of desire or motivation), *comfortable* is 'cheering' (as in the Prayer Book's 'comfortable words'), not 'cosy/snug', *angur* is from Old Norse and is 'trouble/sorrow', *stynted* is 'stopped', *unhappy* is as strong as 'accursed', *ever* is 'always', and *prevy* is 'private/secret'. There is a bad mistake – 'of somer commynge', where the verbal noun in *-ynge* should be preceded by a genitive *someres* ('Do you object to *my* smoking?'); *longe* is OE *gelong* 'dependent'; and *hit* is still clinging to its *h-*.

4 Grammar on the Eve of the Reformation

To take us into the sixteenth century I have chosen a piece of stanzaic poetry (its formal versification may show us which syllables are to be sounded, and whether -*e* has any metrical function), verse of a homely and unsubtle sort, by an old-fashioned man who never came to terms with the Reformation and was successively monk, friar, and London city rector: ALEXANDER BARCLAY (who died old in 1552). His *Life of St George* (1515), being ordinary and not courtly, may best illustrate how the language sounded to undemanding readers; here are lines 1114–1127 and 1163–1169:

> The kynge and quene were chrystenyd firste of all;
>   Next them their doughter gode chaste Alcyone;
> And after them the people great and small
>   Stryvyd who firste myght at the water be,
> 5   Receyvynge baptyme with all humylyte.
>   They were ryght glad to fayth of chryst Jesu
>   With all theyr mynde them gladly to subdue.
>
> By hevynly helpe whan this was past and done,
>   All theyr olde Idollys of fendes infernall
> 10 They threwe to grounde and brake them everychone,
>   And halowyd after the temples of them all
>   In laude and honour of one god immortall.
>   The noble knyght infourmed them lykewyse
>   What ryte of servyce that they shuld exercyse . . .
>
> 15 This done, the kynge and quene went for to mete
>   The noble knyght, with them theyr doughter dere.

    Anone the virgyne downe knelyd at his fete
    With humble herte, with meke and lowly chere,
    And oft hym thankyd with mynde and herte intyer
20   For preservacion of hyr meke innocence.
    The kynge and quene than spake in this sentence:

This should first be read aloud; this will give us a (not quite foolproof) guide to the syllabification. We may assume that Barclay is trying to write regular *rime royal*, the stanza-form made so popular by Chaucer in *Troilus and Criseyde*, with its *ababbcc* rhyme-scheme, its line of five stresses and its iambic movement; strictly, a line must be of one out of only four types:

A   tee túm tee túm tee túm tee túm tee túm
B   túm tee tee túm tee túm tee túm tee túm
C   tee túm tee túm tee túm tee túm tee túm tee
D   túm tee tee túm tee túm tee túm tee túm tee

C and D have 'feminine' rhymes; B and D begin with a trochee, not an iambus, but any other trochee would cause a clash of stresses.

    Now the first line is a serious and pleasing attempt at A; if we accept this, it renders silent and inoperative the *-e* of *quene* (the *-e* of *kynge* and *firste* elide anyway) and either the *-e-* or the final vowel of *chrystenyd*; was it intended as *chryst'nyd* or *chrysten'd*?

    Line 2 is Type B; *gode* must lose its *-e*; the proper name is *Álcyoné*, of three syllables, rhyming with *bē*.

    Line 3 is clear Type A, and 1.4 Type B – provided that we give *Stryvyd* two syllables – and this of course lends colour to the reading *chryst'nyd* in line 1; the final *-e* on *firste* is certainly a casualty.

    Line 5 is slightly broken-backed; since *baptyme* was probably stressed on the second syllable, the *-vyng-* has to be slurred away, the *-e* of *Receyvynge* and *baptyme* doesn't count, and the line goes tee túm tee tee túm tee túm tee túm tee túm, a faulty Type A.

    Lines 6 and 7 are Type A, *Jesú* being stressed on the ultimate and the *-e* of *mynde* not showing a dative or anything else, and so disappearing.

    Line 8 is A, with elision like our own 'heav'nly', and *helpe* is no more a dative than *mynde* was, the *-e* being again silent.

    Line 9 is B, a baddish line where the weak *of* has to bear a stress; *olde* = old', *Idollys* = *Idoll's*, *fendes* = *fend's*; *infernáll*, with its two stresses, is a proper reminder of its French origin. If we have to rescue the line, it can be done only by supposing *Ídoll's of féndes* (for an unstressed *fendes* would be reprehensible), and the pattern túm tee tee túm tee tee túm tee túm tee túm, which is ugly.

Line 10 is straightforward A, and the four -*e* endings are no longer inflexions.

Line 11 is a limping A; *halowyd* = *hal'wyd*, and there is an extra unstressed syllable at -*ter the*, and likewise line 12, with the slur at -*our of*.

Line 13 needs all *infourmed*'s three syllables to make a good A, but this is in line with the full -*yd* of lines 1, 4, 11.

Line 14 is A, with a slur at -*vyce that*.

Lines 15–16 are A, with complete loss of the five -*e* endings (though *noble* is left with two syllables in the way that we still use); so with lines 18 and 21, losing seven -*e* endings but keeping *humble* in the same rhythm as *noble*.

Line 17 is a worry. Even if we suppose *knel'd* (we have now shortened it to *knelt*), the stress pattern will be bad: *down* (an adverb) stressed, *knel'd* (a verb, and the most important word in the line) unstressed, *at* (a mere preposition) stressed. So, once again, I believe in the full reality of -*yd*, though this involves, as before, two unstressed syllables slurring at -*gyne downe* (and the *at* still stressed). And line 19 adds to the worry; I have made out a case for every -*yd* as a syllable, but this would give the line eleven syllables where its type (A) should have only ten – there are no type C or D lines in this extract. A small compromise is needed: I don't believe in *thank'd* here, but allowing yet another pair of unstressed syllables in the middle, -*kyd* and *with*, will again produce the pattern tee túm tee túm tee tee túm tee túm tee túm, a form also arising from the slurred -*cion of* in line 20.

I have required you to work hard and meticulously at the flow of these twenty-one lines, and any reader who is deaf to metre will have found it boring – or a revelation. But we are, in this pedestrian and adequate verse, at an important stage of the language; between those two dozen or so inflexions of the year 1434 in Margery Kempe and Barclay in 1521, there has been such a falling-away that the tally in this archaic-*looking* verse is meagre indeed: the past tense singular of 'weak' verbs in *yd*, the past tense plural likewise, and also the past participle (e.g. *thankyd, Stryvyd, chrystenyd*); the past tense singular of 'weak' verbs in -*ed* (*infourmed*). All these inflexions are complete syllables. Nothing else, here at any rate, remains as far as the ear is a guide; the eye, seeing all the final -*e* conventions, is obviously unreliable. There are still, of course, archaisms – *ryght* 'very' is still familiar in the North; the reflexive *them* in 'to subdue them(selves)' is good Middle English; *brake* is closer to the Old English past tense than our *broke* (which resembles the past participle); in line 14, *What* and *that* make a clumsy construction; *This done* is an 'absolute' of a kind which is now rarer; *for to* is out of favour save in balladry and folk speech, as in *Widdicombe Fair*; *Anone* still meant 'at once', *chere* 'countenance' and *sentence* 'vein'; *spake* is Biblical. Yet the funniest-looking form is now a 'modernizing' one – *Stryved*; this is a strange case, because being a French borrowing it should conform to the regular verbs and have a past tense *strived*, as here, but we forced it into the *drive* conjugation as *strive, strove, striven*, and consider *strived* as a 'wrong' form for the two latter, though the dictionaries allow it as an alternative.

Thus stood English grammar on the eve of the Reformation and in some less precisely datable relationship with the English Renaissance. The language was beginning its 'Modern' period.

Our Retention of Archaic Inflexions

This is probably the most convenient place to consider, without recourse to extended quotation of texts, the buried survival of dead grammar that can still be discovered in our speech and writing. I have already considered the 'weak' plural noun *oxen* and its imitators; the *ge-* of *handiwork*, normally misquoted by people who say 'Summer is a-coming in' (and call the lyric 'Spring Song') when it is actually 'is icumen', meaning *has come* (so it's a 'Summer Song'); the genitive singular without -*s* of a feminine noun, as in *Lady Day* or *Friday*; the uninflected genitive singular of a noun of kinship, as in *mother tongue* and *mother wit*; and the genitive singular of 'weak' nouns as in *Sunday, Monday*.

Other waifs from the Old English noun system include the dative singular in -*e* still holding on in *alive*, 'in life', marking the difference between Middle English *lif* nominative and *live* dative. The dative plural (Old English -*um*) is hardly more vigorous; it is seen in *whilom* 'at whiles' (now 'formerly'), but *seldom* is an odd version of Old English *seldan*; *Byron* 'at the cowsheds' is from -*um*, as in *Hanham* (near Bristol), once *Hanum* 'at the rocks', but very many singular -*e* map-references survive unpronounced in our place-names and therefore in our place-name surnames, and some Devon surnames even retain a pronunciation of it, as in *Forder* 'at the ford'. An Old English genitive plural of 'strong' nouns in *-ra* sleeps like a fly in amber in the obsolete *Childermas* 'the mass of the children' for Holy Innocents' Day (28 December). Some of the old anomalous plurals of the *louse-lice* sort are extinct (*goat*, for instance, is now 'strong'); but *brōc* (I must exceptionally give the vowel its sign of length), meaning a 'trouser', has had a little adventure, with its old plural *brēc* (two legs) made to look more plural as *breeches* and even doubled up again as a *pair of breeches*, the vowel meanwhile being shortened to *britches*. The old instrumental case of the demonstrative/article survives in 'all *the* better' ('better by that much') and '*the* more, *the* merrier'. One other feature of the noun is the suffix *-ster* for feminines, surviving properly only in *spinster* – such forms as the *Brewster Sessions*, and the surnames *Webster* or *Baxter*, being male or epicene.

Among verbs I have given the negative *willy-nilly* its airing, and the Southern present indicative plural in 'Manners makyth man', which has nothing to do with table-manners. The subjunctive, for which I have pleaded plentifully, survives with anyone who ever says *Please* ('if it please you'), or who doesn't like saying 'if I was you', or who votes 'that Joe Bloggs be elected convener', or who bucolically says 'Come Michaelmas'. One real freak refugee from richly inflected times is to *bask*, where the *-sk* goes back to the Middle/Reflexive voice of Old Norse *batha* 'to bath', with the meaning 'to bath oneself'. The old present participle in *-and(e)*, *-end(e)*, *-ind(e)*, which we saw being replaced by the ambiguous *-ing*, is surprisingly dead, save that a Scots regiment has the motto BYDAND 'waiting', and a *sty* on your eye is probably from the mistake *sty-on-eye*, ousting *styan eye*, from Old English *stigend* 'rising, swelling'.

We should at this stage (though it cannot be done exhaustively) add some of the more striking examples of dead but buried syntax, the word as a neighbour. We still find scraps like the 'accusative of reference', in *nothing daunted, nothing lo(a)th*, 'in no respect discouraged /reluctant(ly)'; the inversion of subject and verb to express an *if*-clause in 'were there any reason'; *at* instead of *to* to precede the infinitive, as in *ado*, which can also be 'to-do'; inanimates 'possessing' with a genitive singular *-s*, as in *batsman* or (so they say) *It's early days yet* – 'early of the day'; the 'adverbial genitive' singular, where *-s* on a noun gives it adverbial force, is much commoner than we realise in misspelt words like *once, twice, (whiles* becoming) *whilst*, and clearly expressed in the flavoured phrase *must needs* ('must of necessity').

A pedant should be very careful before he use (subjunctive) the word 'correct' about a construction or an inflection. 'I was given a book' has now its niche in the language, but is patently very wrong indeed: *I* wasn't given at all – a book was, and it was given *me* (dative). 'If I like' is in error, too; *like* meant 'please', and the usage was 'if it like (subjunctive) me'; the same holds good in the indicative – *You like it* should be *It likes you*, but it is too late to go back now. We have noticed old 'strong' verbs becoming regular 'weak'; that was only human, but to make them *irregular* 'weak', with forms like *leapt, wept*, appears no advantage; and the 'weak' have even become 'strong' – *strive*, as we have seen, and *wear*, which was eventually dragged into the *bear* conjugation; *catch*, from French, was oddly made irregular 'weak' instead of *catch-catched-catched*.

5 The Sixteenth Century and Bacon

Barclay looked little like a Renaissance humanist; his contemporary, SIR THOMAS MORE (1478–1535), whose medium was prose, has an altogether more modern look. The English version of his Latin *Utopia* is not his, but we can witness his mature prose in the *History of King Richard III*, a piece of Tudor propaganda powerful yet not unadorned, its word-order contrived for effect. All More's Cockney shrewdness and bluntness, his utter familiarity with Latin, and his devotion to Henry VII and Henry VIII, come out in this book – written by him in Latin and English in the second decade of the 1500s. The language (once the spelling is adjusted to our conventions) is recognisably our own, save for the patches of alliteration like the *l . . .l . . .l . . .r . . .r . . .r . . .t . . .t . . .t . . .* in the first sentence here. The Princes in the Tower have been smothered, buried, exhumed, re-buried and lost.

And thus as I have learnt of[1] them that much knew and little cause had to lie, were these two noble princes, these innocent tender children, born of most royal blood, brought up in great wealth, likely long to live to reign and rule in the realm, by traitorous tyranny taken[2], deprived of their estate, shortly[3] shut up in prison, and privily slain and murdered, their bodies cast God wot[4] where, by the cruel ambition of their unnatural uncle and his dispiteous[5] tormentors. Which things on every part well pondered[6], God never gave this world a more notable example, neither[7] in what unsurety standeth[8] this worldly weal[9], or what mischief worketh[8] the proud enterprise of an[10] high heart, or finally what wretched end ensueth[11] such dispiteous cruelty.

34

1 *from*, followed by two clauses with their verbs post-fixed as in Latin.
2 These nine alliterating words have an inescapably comic sound to our ears.
3 *quickly* rather than *briefly*.
4 *knows*, as in that dire poem that begins 'A garden is a lovesome thing, God wot!' – which by a skilful grammatical trick gives the name to plaster gnomes, windmills, fishermen, and so on, in suburban gardens, 'Godwottery and garden pottery'.
5 *pitiless*.
6 These seven words form a Latinate 'ablative' absolute.
7 Where, by our newish rules against double negatives, we require *either*.
8 The three *-eth* inflexions remind us that one hundred years later the King James Bible still adheres to them.
9 *wealth* and *prosperity*, handily balanced with *woe* by many writers, but now not truly extant even in *commonweal*.
10 The *-n* not now kept before a pronounced *h-*.
11 Influenced, perhaps, by the direct objects of Latin *sequor* and French *suivre*, More omits the usual preposition *on*.

I said that this language, respelt, is 'recognisably our own', but there is a fault: More, the Latinist, does not realise that English has not a great panoply of inflexions to cover that first sentence. What exactly is being said? Thus these child princes were born of the blood royal, brought up, destined to rule, seized, impoverished, incarcerated, secretly butchered, and buried – a catalogue of their lives? Or is it that thus these child princes who *had been* born to better things, were seized, etc. – the contrast of their inheritance and their fate?

From Puritanism encountered at Cambridge, from a later position of moderate Anglicanism, from the need to sing a new era of nationalism and popular personal rule, EDMUND SPENSER (*c.* 1552–1599) oddly chose for his greatest poem – two-thirds of his surviving output – the modes of Chaucer, who died a conventional Roman Catholic, and quite capable of turning a bawdy story, in 1400. The modes were imperfectly grasped, but wonderfully well used; the mighty stanza owed nothing to Chaucer; and the inflexional system was, sensibly, contemporary for the most part. In *The Shepheardes Calender*, Spenser had already experimented with odd speech (after all, the shepherds are conversing on some pretty difficult subjects) in odd metres, and their dialect is plainly seen as needing odd old grammar. Thus in 'September', Diggon says

> Thus chatten the people in theyr steads,
> Ylike as a Monster of many heads.
> But they that shooten nearest the pricke,
> Sayne, other the fat from their beards doen lick.
> For bigge bulles of *Basan* brace hem about,
> That with theyr hornes butten the more stoute:
> But the leane soules treaden underfoote.
> And to seeke redresse mought little boote:
> For liker bene they to pluck away more,
> Then ought of the gotten good to restore.

This is inconsistently Chaucerian – the 3rd person plural present indicatives in -*n* will do quite well (*chatten*, *shooten*, *sayne* t an -*e*, *doen* very inventive, *butten* – then why not *bracen*? –, *treaden*, *bene*); but the infinitives *lick*, *seeke*, *pluck*, *restore*, have no -*en*; the past participle *gotten* has one – as it still has in America. The 3rd person plural pronoun is shown inconsistently – *they*, *hem*, *their*/*theyr* for Chaucer's *h*- forms. The vocabulary gives the right atmosphere: *steads* for 'places', *Ylike* as if from a *ge*- form, *mought* for the past tense of *may*, *boote* for 'remedy'. The final -*e* 'inflexions' are mere decoration: *bigge* is not a plural adjective, *stoute* not an adverb, or any such thing.

Yet the same Eclogue, which is somewhat free from supposedly classical intricacies of the 'oaten reed' type, experiments comically with dialect:

> HOBBINOL: Diggon Davie, I bidde her good day:
>   Or Diggon her is, or I missaye.
> DIGGON: Her was her, while it was daye light,
>   But now her is a most wretched wight.
>   For day, that was, is wightly past,
>   And now at earst the dirke night doth hast.

Nobody ever talked like this; the all-purposes pronoun 'her' is, admittedly, still heard in our worst slang, but *day*/*daye* gives the measure of this language, and otherwise what is achieved comes from dying words like *wightly* and *dirke* (*wight* itself occurs even in Shakespeare – there are 'fairest wights' in a sonnet).

The 10th Eclogue ('October') is a consistently deliberate imitation of older English, and long enough to grow painful. The poet Cuddie complains (*ll.* 13–15):

> The dapper dainties that I wont devise,
> To feede youthes fancie, and the flocking fry,
> Delighten much: what I the bett for thy?

This is more Chaucerian than is good for it, with added titbits: three alliterations in the first line, four in the second; *wont* for 'used to', *dapper* for 'pretty', and *fry* for 'swarm, crowd'; the 3rd person plural marked in *delighten*, but meaningless and silent *-e* on *feede* and *fancie* and in *youthes*; *bett* is the old adverb meaning 'better'; above all, *for thy* is Middle English *forthy*, 'for that', remembering the Old English instrumental case. Since Spenser has not fully mastered this language – or is letting it develop and modernise itself – we shall find errors or modifications like line 24, 'Whereto thou list their trayned wiles entice.' Here *trayned* keeps its *e* and so its second syllable, but *list* has become personal instead of remaining impersonal as *thee list*. The stanza formed by lines 31–36 has four *-n* inflexions for the present plural verb, another *for thy*, one *-eth* for the present singular verb – but *rewards* and *feedes* as well. The reflexive *Turne thee* (line 40) is convincing, but four lines after it has *-selfe* added in *stretch herselfe*; then at once:

> Whither thou list in fayre Elisa rest,
> Or if thee please in bigger notes to sing –

thou list, modernised personal, but *thee please*, archaic impersonal. One archaism perhaps led to another, so that *yclad in claye* (line 61) is followed in the next line by *long ygoe*. The subjunctive appears to be for occasional use; so in line 80 Poetry is asked where her 'place' is

> If not in Princes pallace thou *doe* sitt . . . [subjunctive]
> Ne brest of baser birth *doth* thee embrace [indicative]

But *The Faerie Queene* was in preparation, and its demands on language were utterly different, though equally archaic words ensued. Carpet knights who often need courage and a strong arm

have rum adventures cast in an appropriate vocabulary; but the
obsolete words and the nostalgic outlook matter less than the well
recaptured cadences and melodies of Chaucer, including vitally some
unstressed and tripping inflexions, as in 'As whilome was the antique
worldes guize' (I l.st.39), where (unfortunately) we are not directed to
dock the -*e* on *whilome* or *antique*, but only to sound the -*es* of *worldes*
separately. Though Spenser does his duty by retaining -*eth* so often, it
is noticeable that even in the stateliest lines the -*s* will occur instead; in
stanza 36 of the poem, a mid-line *creepeth* gives promise of sonorous
music, but the plural noun *liddes* enforces the verb forms *biddes* and
riddes, and *kindes* and *mindes* enforce *findes*. That foolish state of affairs
whereby

>   The boy sings

but   The boys sing

is here taking its toll, and the result is ugly to the ear. Spenser also
coined (unless we have lost his sources) *daint* as an adjective and *cherry*
('cheer') as a verb; with this polite form of cheating, and so many
other stocks of words, it is surprising that he so often adjusts the
language into a paradigm of inversion, Latinate relative pronouns,
and all the constructions that keep such a brake on the poem. The
30th stanza plods typically:

> He faire[1] the knight saluted, louting[2] low,
>   Who faire[1] him quited[3], as that courteous was[4]:
> And after asked him, if he did know
>   Of straunge adventures, which abroad did pas[5].
>   Ah, my deare Sonne (quoth he), how should, alas
>   Silly[6] old man, that lives in hidden cell,
>   Bidding his beades all day for his trespas,
>   Tydings of warre and worldly trouble tell?
> With holy father sits[7] not with such things to mell[8].

1 Adverb in -*e*? (but not sounded, anyway).
2 'bowing'.
3 'repaid his greeting'.
4 'being courteous'.
5 'were happening'.
6 'simple'.
7 'is becoming, suits'.
8 'mingle, meddle'.

The grammar is simple, ours, except that *askèd* must have two syllables; the syntax is tortuous; the diction quaint in places; and the whole stanza helps to substantiate Ben Jonson's statement that through aping the ancients Spenser 'writ no language'. The poetasters who followed Chaucer said that *he* had 'sugared' and 'enamelled' our language, as if he had put the pretty and figurative bits on like icing, and that he had 'illumined' it 'with flowers of rhetoric'; and the aureate diction and constructions, that followed from this attitude, reached Spenser still undiscredited. Words like *ywis* 'certainly' (from Old English *gewiss*) and *eftsoons* lingered on and became a bad pattern; and did everyone know what they meant? – those who wrote and printed *Y wis* certainly didn't.

When, hundreds of pages on, we have thought and fought our way through this colossal and still truncated poem, and reached the second and final stanza of the 'unperfite' last scrap of the Mutability Cantos, the linguistic atmosphere all at once becomes strangely fresh and clear. It will look even clearer with modernized spelling:

> Then gin I think on that which Nature said [long vowel]
>   Of that same time when no more Change shall be,
> But steadfast rest of all things firmly stayed
>   Upon the pillars of Eternity,
>   That is contrare to Mutability:
>   For all that moveth doth in Change delight:
> But thenceforth all shall rest eternally
>   With him that is the God of Sabaoth hight:
> O that great Sabaoth God, grant me that Sabaoth's sight.

The form *gin* was not an abbreviation of *begin*, *contrare* sounds straight out of French, and *hight* (which was originally a passive verb 'was called' – or, admittedly, the past participle 'called') is not here passive voice without the *is* to go with it. Yet, with so much that is modern, one piece of older syntax adheres – that *Sabaoth's sight* is 'sight of that Sabaoth', where the 'possessive' -*s* would now be impossible.

I could choose from his *Essays* more winsome passages of FRANCIS BACON (1561–1626) than this rather contorted piece (I viii 1) of *The Advancement of Learning* (1605):

And for magnitude, as Alexander the Great, after that he was used to great armies, and the great conquests of the spacious provinces in Asia, when he received letters out of Greece, of some fights and services there, he said, It seemed to him that he was advertised of the battles of the frogs and the mice, that the old tales went of. So certainly, if a man meditate much upon the universal frame of nature, the earth with men upon it (the divineness of souls except) will not seem much other than an ant-hill, whereas some ants carry corn, and some carry their young, and some go empty, and all to and fro a little heap of dust.

It is illuminating to see a great genius, skilled in Latin scholarship and expression, making something of a botch of his native language: clauses heaped up, but hardly in a Classical 'period' structure; ugly anti-climaxes of monosyllables like *went of*; repetitions like *Alexander . . . he*; Latinisms like that post-fixed *except* (a pretended 'ablative' absolute, *having been excepted*); loose application of prepositions, like the opening *for magnitude* (= ? 'as for magnitude'); the sudden recourse to little native words, where the contrast is too great for an easy transition between the styles – *that the old tales went of*. Yet this last feature can be used with power here; the pomp of Alexander, the drums and tramplings, are marvellously reduced at the end not only by the comparison of humankind with ants but by those last thirty-odd words of colloquial ease and not from the Latin word-stock. Grammatically, we are on familiar ground, though the introductory words *after that* (our 'after') and *whereas* (our 'where', with no idea of contrast) hold us up for a moment, and we notice that *fro* is not the adverb fossilised in the one phrase 'to and fro', but a preposition (now always 'from'); there is only one clear *inflexion* to remind us of our lost grammar, the present subjunctive singular *meditate*.

6   Shakespeare

It would obviously be unwise to treat WILLIAM SHAKESPEARE (1564–1616) as a typical writer of his age, but he must have an emphatic place in the sequence that we are building up, as the author who supremely took the language and accepted its Englishness, but also adapted it and broke its bounds, using one part of speech as if it were another, and even – almost for the first time in our literature – using a contrived cacophony, here to enact the chaos in Macbeth's polity, 'Now minutely revolts upbraid his faith-breach'. He was never, of course, so vain or so reactionary as to lay down guide-lines for his successors; he had been given a grammar school education, and he was aware of how pedants and highly trained linguists could talk – like those old bores Holofernes and Nathaniel in *Love's Labour's Lost*, just as he was obviously aware of a colourful range of ordinary and even rough speech. He had a gift for parody, and mere imitation of these idioms was a resource on which he could always draw; but he knew that the most telling idiom of drama is neither the dully repeated demotic nor the flashily enhanced rhetorical, but is its own self – is a language perpetually coming into being, a language of reply and of the unfinished, with the unexpected and the potential burning within it. More than in any other kind of poetry, it has never been said before; the weapons of the protagonists furnish it, the dramatic strangeness of the scene demands it, and since it cannot be the duty of any playwright to create a dull and merely realistic 'confrontation', the language will happen with the events, though shackled by that five-stress line of iambic movement. This was a discipline relaxed only when a character fell into prose, or when there were stanzaic songs, or when Nathaniel, in his third speech, uses three couplets of Ogden Nash verse, with pure rhymes but a syllable pattern of 16, 21, 17, 15, 15, 12.

The best available book on *Shakespeare's Language* is called just that

41

and is by Professor N. F. Blake (Macmillan, 1983). It is not dressed up with the vocabulary of modern linguistics, and its richly illustrated chapters on nouns and verbs (and their phrasal equivalents) are rounded off with an excellent treatment of those little parts of speech which are so hard to describe excitingly – adverbs, prepositions and conjunctions. I may best continue with the method I have been using, and exhibit various passages from young and unfamiliar, or mature and oft-quoted, plays. Since this first excerpt did not appear to me to require the original spelling, I offer it respelt from its 1590–91 form, perhaps not all by Shakespeare; it is, to the reader's surprise, *King Henry the Sixth, Part III*, II v, and poor King Henry, mooching on the battlefield of Towton, can do nothing but soliloquise:

> This battle fares like to the morning's war,
> When dying clouds contend with growing light,
> What time the shepherd, blowing of his nails,
> Can neither call it perfect day nor night . . .
> 5 So is the equal poise of this fell war.
> Here on this molehill will I sit me down.
> To whom God will, there be the victory!
> For Margaret my queen, and Clifford too,
> Have chid me from the battle; swearing both
> 10 They prosper best of all when I am thence . . .
> O God! methinks it were a happy life,
> To be no better than a homely swain . . .
> Gives not the hawthorn-bush a sweeter shade
> To shepherds looking on their silly sheep,
> 15 Than doth a rich-embroider'd canopy
> To kings that fear their subjects' treachery? . . .
> And to conclude, – the shepherd's homely curds,
> His cold thin drink out of his leather bottle,
> His wonted sleep under a fresh tree's shade,
> 20 All which secure and sweetly he enjoys,
> Is far beyond a prince's delicates,
> His viands sparkling in a golden cup,
> His body couched in a curious bed,
> When care, mistrust, and treason waits on him.

Let us first consider the syntax of this passage – not daring or pliant, but in places certainly not yet ours. Inanimate nouns occur as 'possessing' with the genitive's; *morning's* and *tree's*, where we prefer to use *of*. In line 3, *What time* is a Latinism resembling *Quo tempore* 'at which time'; and blowing *of* one's fingernails is now as unfamiliar as looking *on* sheep, rather than *after* them – good examples of the need for Blake's chapter on the innocuous-looking little words. We can rationally object to line 4, where *neither can . . . nor night* is not the right parallel: 'Can call it neither perfect day nor night' is required. In line 6 *me* is reflexive – 'myself'. *To whom God will* in line 7 is Latinate again, and *will* may be an intended subjunctive (involving the sense 'To whomever'), followed by the subjunctive *be*, with the sense 'Let the victory be with whichever one God may want'. The adverb *thence* in line 10 has adjectival force, 'when I am away from there'. Then *methinks* is the mediaeval 'it seems to me' (dative), and *were* is past subjunctive singular used conditionally, 'it would be'. The question in lines 13–16 is neatly asked in a way now closed to us, since we must say 'Does not the hawthorn-bush give . . .', though we pretend to have a dative when we use the formula 'Doesn't the hawthorn-bush give the shepherd . . . a sweeter shade?' In line 20 we would tend to start with 'All *of* which', and to regard *secure and sweetly* as a jumble of adjective and adverb (with one 'right' and the other 'wrong', but Shakespeare in *Richard II* describes Norfolk, or qualifies his action, with a similar amalgam *sprightfully and bold*); likewise, we don't like modifying *embroider'd* with an adjective, and demand *richly*. The *is* at the start of line 21 would now be frowned on as having three subjects, and this 'error' is repeated at the end with three subjects of the verb *is* instead of *are*.

These nineteen differences from our syntax in a mere 24 lines are the really noteworthy area of this passage; compared with them, the inflexional system offers no puzzle whatever – the three subjunctives (whose occurrence the previous paragraph explains); the irregular 'weak' past participle *chid* (familar in a nursery tag, 'speak when you're spoken to, sulk when you're chid') from *chide*, which also has the participle *chidden*; the three required syllables of *embroider'd* need the apostrophe to prevent its having four, whereas the poet needs two in *couched* and so spells it out in full (*wonted*, of course, cannot be elided into one). The final threat to the *-th* inflexion of the 3rd personal singular present indicative is seen in the equivocal forms *fares*, *gives*, *doth*, *enjoys*, *waits*: only the auxiliary *doth* keeps the pretty inflexion (as it still occasionally did in the first edition of the *Encyclopaedia Britannica*, as if more polite).

There have been ten clear changes in the meanings of words, that least of our concerns in this book: *fares* is here 'proceeds'; *perfect*, 'absolute'; *swain* 'boy, servant'; *silly* 'innocent, simple'; *delicates*, 'delicacies'; *viands* now merely facetious; *couched* 'bedded, lying down', because a couch is a sofa now; *curious* 'skilfully made'; *care*, 'worry'; *waits on* 'attends, hangs around' – not like a waiter at table. Thus in this introduction to Shakespeare's language we see that what most separates him from us is his syntax, idioms, constructions; his semantic differences are at least ten-fold and sometimes surprising; the grammar, accidence, inflexions, are hardly an obstacle. But will this be the pattern in the mature Shakespeare?

A Midsummer Night's Dream (*c*. 1595) should prove a good place to find various idioms: Theseus, and his subjects in his presence, with their stately speech; the young aristocrats talking among themselves, mainly of Love; and the 'rude mechanicals, That work for bread upon Athenian stalls'. In the latter part of Act I, Scene i, it becomes quite obvious – and not very creditable to Shakespeare – that he uses *-th* or *-s* for the 3rd person singular present indicative according to how many syllables he wants, when Hermia says

The more I hate, the more he follows me,

and Helena replies

The more I love, the more he hateth me.

It is much the same with the old 'weak' *-n* plural of nouns: Helena in her first speech envies Hermia's eyes, Hermia says that she and Lysander will turn their eyes away from Athens, Helena when alone says that Demetrius dotes on Hermia's eyes, that Love doesn't look with the eyes, and that Cupid has no eyes, but that Demetrius was first unfaithful when he 'look'd on Hermia's *eyne*' to rhyme with *mine*. This 'look'd on' is the rule; the conversation of the three young people produces *Seem'd, turn'd, devis'd, wing'd, beguil'd, perjur'd, look'd, hail'd, dissolv'd*, with no trace of a true *-ed* if the stem of a verb can fuse with the dental inflexion. Shakespeare's ear tells him that the auxiliary *does* (however pronounced – they say *dooz* in Bristol) is an ugly, low-browed little word, and *doth* remains frequent – twice in a six-line speech by Lysander; *hath* occurs twice, with no trace of *has*.

In the 72 lines from the entry of Helena to the end of the scene, this is the small tally of inflexions needing comment, apart from the

inflexionless 3rd person singular present subjunctive; but the syntactical features – especially the subjunctives – are less familiar. The
unloved Helena tells Hermia 'Demetrius loves your fair' – the
adjective taking over the function of the noun. Successively, in her
first speech, she uses 'O were favour so . . . ere I go [where the force is
felt as subjunctive, though the inflexion doesn't convey it] . . . Were
the world mine'. She is at the moment an uncertain, tentative lady:
'would that fault were mine!'. Hermia and Lysander, happy in their
love, just use to her the two prayerful subjunctives 'good luck grant
thee thy Demetrius!' and 'Demetrius dote on you!'. Hermia's greeting
to her 'Whither away?' assumes a verb of motion, as in our jesting 'I
must away', and her immediate answer 'Call you me fair?' is blest
with that purity of construction which is now forbidden to us – so that
we say 'Do you call me?' or 'Are you calling me?' In 'your tongue's
melody' the inanimate tongue 'possesses' with an -*s*. The lovers 'will
fly this place' with no preposition to intervene. Hermia's quickly
repeated phrasing, 'I did Lysander see' and 'what graces in my love
do dwell', is as ugly as the modern tyranny of *do* over our verbs, and
her lover uses it twice immediately after. Here is 'you and I . . . were
wont to lie', going back to Old English *wunian* 'to dwell, be
accustomed' and still clinging on in our facetious 'olde' speech; but we
are afraid of it, not knowing whether to make it long (as if it were the
same as *won't*) or short. Left to herself, Helena tries to cheer herself by
argument, and shows some rhetorical skill, pointing her contrasts
very neatly and of course having available the tight construction
'Demetrius thinks not so'. We have also lost 'I will go tell him', though
people still shout 'Go fetch!' to their dogs. But we have improved on
'his sight', where we have opened the phrase out from a possible
meaning 'the vision which he possesses' to '(my) sight of him', the
partitive construction.

In all this quicksilver conversation, only *fair* 'beautiful', *favour*
'looks', *bated* 'excepted', *other-some* 'some others' (obviously), *waggish*
'mischevious', and *intelligence* 'information', require the glossary. The
pattern evolves, therefore, of few inflexions and diminished lexical
difficulties, but abundant archaisms of syntax.

Four years later, *Julius Caesar* appeared; it was deemed an 'easy'
play at school, and was no doubt a mine of missed nuances. As a
warning against hasty reading, I have often quoted the end of
Cassius's first big speech against Caesar,

> Ye gods, it doth amaze me
> A man of such a feeble temper should
> So get the start of the majestic world,
> And bear the palm alone.

(Act I, Sc.ii)

If I may just ask some questions about this, instead of offering answers as well, it will suggest the magnitude of our responsibility in proposing to read Shakespeare: How serious is *Ye Gods*? – it is always facetious with *us*, so is this use of it contemptuous or awestruck? Why *doth*? – the more colloquial *does* was available, and (though they would infringe the metre) *amazeth* and *amazes*. How figurative is *amaze*? – does Cassius feel as if he were in a labyrinth, or is he just very surprised? Is it slangy to leave out the connective *that* before *A man*? (Chaucer omitted it often, even at the most solemn junctures). Is *feeble* just 'shaky, weak', or does *febrile* 'feverish' come into it? – Caesar had the falling-sickness. (They explained *temper* – and only *temper* – in school, defining it as *temperament* or *constitution*). Has *should* any sense of compulsion, of *ought to*? How newly metaphorical was the sporting figure of getting a start and winning the palm? – and was *bearing* a palm a little too stately (for wearing or carrying), as if the Palm Sunday procession, or a martyr's effigy, had rubbed off on to it? If you find this kind of close reading a drudgery, give up Shakespeare, or realise that you are reading him only in the form Shown To The Children.

When Casca starts talking, we have already been warned that he is 'sour' but frank; his account of the attempted crowning of Caesar is indeed casual and sneering, but is surely to be read as a shrewd sizing-up of what has happened, and its prose releases it for his type of rhetoric.

> Why, there was a crown offer'd him [even in prose, this elision is incorporated in the spelling]; and being offer'd him [this participle 'dangles' between *crown* and the oncoming *he*], he put it by [which is *not* 'he stored it up'] with the back of his hand, thus; and then the people fell a-shouting [formerly *on* + the verbal noun].
> (BRUTUS: Was the crown offer'd him thrice?)
> Ay, marry [an oath by the Blessed Virgin Mary], was't [not asking a question], and he put it by thrice [I hope we shall retain the services of *thrice* – but, now I come to think of it, I have never used it

in speech], every time gentler [tut-tut! this should be *more gently*] than other [Middle English would have had *the other* for 'the next after' or 'the next before'; *other*, by itself, remains strange]; and at every putting-by [a well used and pithy verbal noun] mine [the form in use before a vowel or silent *h*-] honest neighbours shouted . . .

I can as well be hang'd [again, the determination that it isn't hangèd] as tell the manner of it; it was mere foolery; I did not mark ['observe, watch'] it. I saw Mark Anthony offer him a crown; – yet 'twas [still, for instance, regular Devon use] not a crown neither [we now insist on *either*], 'twas one of these [a use of the demonstrative hard to justify, since no such coronet is present] coronets; and, as I told you, he put it by once; but, for all that, to my thinking, he would fain [*glad(ly)*] have had it. Then he offer'd it to him again; then he put it by again: but, to my thinking, he was very loth to lay his fingers off it [we keep only the idiom *on it*]. And then he offer'd it the third time; he put it the third time by [we prefer to keep the weak little *by* earlier in the sentence, where it can bear less emphasis]; and still as he refused it, the rabblement [a colder and more sarcastic form than a concrete word] shouted, and clapp'd their chopp'd [chapp'd] hands, and threw up their sweaty night-caps, and utter'd such a deal of stinking breath because Caesar refused the crown, that it had almost choked [? *it almost choked, it could have almost choked*] Caesar; for he swounded [like Coleridge's archaism for the noun *swoon*, in 'The Ancient Mariner'], and fell down at it; and for my own part, I durst [that fine Bristolism for *dared*] not laugh, for fear of opening my lips and receiving the bad air . . .

If the tag-rag [also *rag-tag and bobtail*] people did not clap him and hiss him, according as he pleased them and displeased them, as they use to [*are accustomed* – we keep only its past tense, which we pronounce *ewster*] do the players [*actors*] in the theatre, I am no true man . . . He pluck'd me ['I' have nothing to do with the action, really, and *me* is just an expletive like *if you please* or *would you believe it?*] ope [as so often, the loss – temporary in *this* case – of a final -*n*] his doublet, and offer'd them his throat to cut.

(Act I, Sc. ii)

Racy and reciprocal (Casca answers the questions fired at him), this raconteur's English, and his humour that sees the silly and self-deceiving aspects of human nature, is at once communicable; my notes were only to put the final polish on our understanding.

When, later in the play, the sophist Artemidorus is drawing up his written warning to Caesar, he includes one serious lapse into illiteracy: 'If thou beest not immortal, look about you'. (Act II, Sc. iii) A subjunctive *be* after an *if* would be expected; but the mixture of the familiar singular *thou/thee* and the polite plural *ye/you* is very surprising. Not that Shakespeare is over-careful here; in *King Henry the Eighth* (1612–13), he – or whoever wrote this bit – lets Wolsey say, in Act III, Scene ii,

> Vain pomp and glory of this world, I hate ye.

It is as if *ye* is so undermined that it is thought to be the accusative, instead of *you*, or that the doomed *thee* (the accusative singular) is coming to be confused with this nominative plural, object for subject, and both to live on only in the great Church masterpieces of 1611 and 1662.

Troilus and Cressida (1601–2), a difficult and harsh play throughout, has many lines of the 'What ho! Rinaldo, lo the hornèd moon' type, not unexpected from all the plumed warriors strutting about; it has some nicely-handled desultory conversation; and in the sudden degeneracy and death of the good Hector is the keenest woe of any of Shakespeare's tragedies. Its vocabulary, and its second tier of vocabulary occasioned by its many metaphors, are quite unpredictable; no line, perhaps, is as strange as Macbeth's

> The multitudinous seas incarnadine,
> Making the green one red,
>
> (*Macbeth*, Act II, Sc. ii)

but Agamemnon before Achilles's tent starts with monosyllables and develops into oddity:

> Let it be known to him that we are here.
> He shent our messengers; and we lay [present tense] by
> Our appertainments, visiting of him.
>
> (*Troilus and Cressida*, Act II, Sc. iii)

We are still making mistakes in our grammar of *lay–laid*, *lie–lay*, but this present tense of *lay* is correct; the past tense of *shend* (a good Old English verb for 'rebuke') has an apt sound; *visiting of him* is like Henry VI's shepherd's *blowing of his nails*; but those proud *appertainments* belong squarely in the pomp of Agamemnon's mind. Cressida, told by Pandarus to 'be moderate', comes out with

> Why tell you me of moderation?
> The grief is fine, full, perfect, that I taste,
> And violenteth in a sense as strong
> As that which causeth it: how can I moderate it?
> If I could temporize with my affection,
> Or brew it to a weak and colder palate,
> The like allayment could I give my grief:
> My love admits no qualifying dross;
> No more my grief, in such a precious loss.
>
> (Troilus and Cressida, Act IV, Sc. iv)

Simple frankness, and a lovely sustained parallel of love and grief, but studded with big words; and the extra bit of dignity is in the grammar of that *-eth* in *violenteth* and *causeth*. Between a sick comedy, or futile tragedy, such as *Troilus* and the real comedy of *As You Like It* is a generation gap of attitude; yet *As You Like It* is only two years older. The many witty exchanges in *Troilus* will come to nothing; the blameless little arguments in Arden are eternally funny:

> JAQUES: Rosalind is your love's name?
> ORLANDO: Yes, just.
> JAQUES: I do not like her name.
> ORLANDO: There was no thought of pleasing you when she was christen'd.
>
> (Act III, Sc. ii)

Such plain words, of course, will far more rarely find a place in the rather sour plays of plot and intrigue like *Measure for Measure*; there is a sinister, close, sticky feeling to the verse in which Isabella describes to the Duke Angelo's plans for her seduction that night:

> He hath a garden circummured with brick,
> Whose western side is with a vineyard back'd;

And to that vineyard is a planched gate,
That makes his opening with this bigger key:
This other doth command a little door
Which from the vineyard to the garden leads;
There have I made my promise [2 of these 3 lines are defective]
Upon the heavy middle of the night
To call upon him. [Will she find her way?, asks
   the Duke]
I have ta'en a due and wary note upon't:
With whispering and most guilty diligence,
In action all of precept, he did show me
The way twice o'er. [Anything else 'greed?, asks
   the Duke]
No, none, but only a repair i' the dark;
And that I have possess'd him my most stay
Can be but brief; for I have made him know
I have a servant comes with me along,
That stays upon me; whose persuasion is
I come about my brother.

                    (Act IV, Sc. i)

Isabella does not talk here like a novice nun; in the latter part of her speech she sounds, with her clipped *ta'en, upon't, o'er, i'*, and her studied deceit, more like a conspirator (which at this point she *is*). Yet her words are not plain; however short most of them are, they are manipulated in a way that gives them new relationships with words as short. Grammatically, there is plenty, but nothing special at all: *hath*, *doth*, the last of the common -*th* inflexions in English, and the rest *makes, leads, comes, stays*; *Whose* not now wholly favoured as the relative pronoun for an inanimate in the genitive (I incline to use it, not 'of which the'); *back'd* and *possess'd*, but *circummured*, and *planched* 'made of planks' shown as having two syllables; *his* for *its* (and, please, not for the increasingly popular *it's*, which = *it is*); *ta'en* has a decided Scots or Northern balladry sound – 'O, they have ta'en my love away'; *most* is good Tudor use for *very* (whereas now we associate 'That's most kind of you' with gush); the auxiliaries (line-fillers, really!) *did* and *doth* are used; *most* for *biggest/longest*, as with the many villages in England like Much Marcle, where *Much* is the positive and means *Big*; between *servant* and *comes* an expected relative was not needed from Chaucer's time onwards, though I am uneasy without it; *comes with me along* looks forward to Herrick's promise to the daffodils that 'we / Will go with you along'; the relative *whose*, after a firm semi-colon, is Latinate (from *cuius*) and would be clearer as *and his*. The semantics are simpler than hitherto, if we are willing mentally to 'translate' *circummured* (think of immured in this conventual context), *repair* (with its misleading glumness of DIY and inert cars), *possess'd* 'put it into his head', *but* 'only', *stays upon* 'attends', *persuasion* 'conviction, assumption'. I have lumped the syntax with the grammar, so little is there of it; and in fact the pattern of this passage varies from our other Shakespeare citations.

Our last illustration from his plays had better be in the oldest recoverable spelling, the text of the 1623 Folio, though this late romance, *The Winter's Tale*, of which this is Act IV, Scene i, lines 36*ff*., was written in 1610–11. I have even left the *u* for *v* and the *v* for *u*, which I spared you in the Middle English passages. The King of Bohemia and his faithful Camillo are about to discover Prince Florizel's plan to marry apparently beneath him:

> POLIXENES: I haue considered so much (Camillo) and with some care, so farre, that I haue eyes vnder my seruice, which looke vpon his remouednesse: from whom I haue this Intelligence, that he is seldome from the house of a most homely shepheard: a man (they say) that from very nothing, and beyond the imagination of his neighbors, is growne into an vnspeakable estate.
>
> CAMILLO: I haue heard (sir) of such a man, who hath a daughter of most rare note: the report of her is extended more, then can be thought to begin from such a cottage.
>
> POLIXENES: That's likewise part of my Intelligence: but (I feare) the Angle that pluckes our sonne thither. Thou shalt accompany vs to the place, where we will (not appearing what we are) haue some question with the shepheard; from whose simplicity, I thinke it not vneasie to get the cause of my sonnes resort thether. 'Prethe be my present partner in this busines, and lay aside the thoughts of Sicillia.
>
> CAMILLO: I willingly obey your command.
>
> POLIXENES: My best *Camillo*, we must disguise our selues.

Since this is nearly Shakespeare's swan-song, it will be nice to see on what linguistic terms we part with him. The spelling (*thither* and *thether*, *remouednesse* but *busines*, *then* for *than*) does not concern us; nor does the strange punctuation (Camillo addressed in brackets or italics; asides or the dropped voice put into brackets like *they say, sir, I feare* – the last very strange, since it is the subject and verb of its little sentence; *'Prethe* 'I pray thee' carefully started with an apostrophe for an omission). The King of course calls the courtier *thee* by right, the courtier responds with *your* correctly. In the vocabulary, 'seldom away from the house' would be a modern 'improvement', *unspeakable* has nothing horrid about it, *note* is 'reputation', *Angle* is 'fishing-rod', and *uneasy* is 'difficult' not 'troubled'. Finally, *most* is holding on to the meaning 'very' and 'My best Camillo' is not to suggest that he has other inferior Camilli.

7 Popular Rhetoric: the Language of Funerary Inscriptions

The English of FUNERARY INSCRIPTIONS has varied from a noble reticence to garrulousness; it is interesting in charting the development of a popular dignified utterance, stratified of course according to society but available to all. Its poor relics are the *In Memoriam* notices in newspapers – 'The pearly gates opened / And in walked Mum', or 'Just gone to God's great garden / And left the door ajar' – a telling reflection on the decline in faith, taste, and sensibility. When Lionel Tollemache of Helmingham, Suffolk, who died *c*. 1550, was finally commemorated, his descendant assumed that people wanted to know *this* kind of thing. By now the year was 1615:

> Baptized Lyone Tollemache my Name
> Since Normans Conquest of unsoyled Fame
> Shews my Descent from Ancestors of Worth;
> And that my Life might not belye my Birth,
> Their Virtues Track with heedful steps I trod,
> Rightful to Men, Religious towards God.
>
> Train'd in the Law, I gain'd the Bar and Bench,
> Not bent to Kindle Strife, but rather Quench;
> Gentle to Clients, in my Counsels Just,
> With Norfolk's Great Duke in no little Trust.
> Sir Joyce his heir was my Fair Faithful Wife;
> Bently my Seat, and Sev'nty Years my Life.

This is in a sensible, shorthand style, with sentences mattering less and strings of attributes forming the pattern. The *-ed* inflexion is still

53

wholly real, so *Baptized* and *unsoyled* have three syllables each, and *Train'd* and *gain'd* must be so spelt if they are to have only one. No sign is given (and historically, why should it be?) that Virtues is genitive 'Virtue's', but a very wrong sign is added to make Sir Joyce genitive, with *his* for the apostrophe *s*. Numerous hack poets must have been able to produce this stuff, sometimes in a blithe and sociable mood, as here, sometimes dolorous. At Collingbourne Ducis, in Wiltshire, the little son of the Earl of Hertford is assessed thus in his epitaph of 1631:

> Speechless tho' yet he were, say all we can
> That saw, he promise did a hopefull man.
> Such fame of body, such a holy soule,
> Argu'd him written in the long liv'd roule.
> But now wee see, by such an infant's losse,
> All are but infant hopes, which death may crosse.

The inversion in the first two lines is grotesque; the 17 words as they stand *ought* to be in the order 7 8 10 11 9 6 12 14 13 15 16 17 2 4 5 3 1. The spellings *Argu'd* and *liv'd* are genuine necessities here, and the past subjunctive singular *were* duly follows *tho'*, which is still pretending to mask a more complicated sound. The *infant's losse* is, of course, not a possessive expression, but the *loss of the infant*.

The little girl's question to her father in the churchyard, 'Daddy, where were all the nasty ones buried?', colours our reading of most epitaphs. But it is still possible for the sceptic to be silenced in the presence of searing grief couched in exquisite words, especially when the setting is a master-carving in an ancient church. All these elements come together (and nowhere better) at Ashbourne in Derbyshire, where Thomas Banks's masterpiece in white marble depicts the nine-year-old Penelope Boothby, who died in 1791; she lies innocently asleep, and the English inscription simply says:

> She was in form and intellect most exquisite.
> The unfortunate Parents ventured their all
> on this frail Bark. And the loss was total.

This, of course, has Taste, which is now a less approved commodity; but we commend even less the big boast of moral or religious qualities. So Catherine Parminter, buried at Ilfracombe in Devon in 1660, has been given a lot to live up to:

Never was Innocence & Prudence Soe lovely,
that had you known her conversation, you
would have said, she was the daughter of
Eve before she eated of the Apple. She hath left
her name.

That first *was* should be *were* to cover the two abstract nouns; the inverted *had you* can still in Modern English cover the meaning of *if*; *eated* was one of several variant forms of the past tense of *eat*; and *hath* (like *doth*) remains fairly vigorous into the eighteenth century.

Realism has always been acceptable, however, and a fine eloquence on the subject of death distinguishes many tombstones even in the most rustic parts; if only they would always stick to prose! – for practised dignity or simple compilation, it has none of the blandishments of verse, or its tags, or its self-satisfied rounding-off of the verse as if something final could be said. The Bible, of course, proved to be the natural quarry for phrases with cadence and with awe-inspiring firmness, the answer to any murmur or to any foolish hope, the justification of the mourner's hope and faith when they are grounded in Christ. Such a use of the Bible is seen on a sailor's memorial at Sancreed in Cornwall, dated 1825:

Occupying his business in great waters he saw the wonders of the Lord and served Him with reverence. Yet that God, whose the sea is, and He made it, hath turned the floods into a wilderness and called him away early to the city of the silent. Thus hath the grave one example more of the mysteries of providence, and to the living is repeated the awful lesson that the race is not to the swift nor the battle to the strong, that firm principles and active piety are no safeguards from the vicissitudes of our lot, that youth shall faint and the young men fall. But they that wait upon the Lord shall renew their strength and mount up on wings as of eagles in that great day.

The Bible lies within every great phrase there; yet it is all clear, serene, human, not antiquated and not pleading as if for a dead faith. The further English Christians turn from the King James Bible and the Book of Common Prayer, the less they will be able to write like this or even to comprehend it; the epitaph of this poor sailor is of a piece with the resounding words to Sir Robert Shirley, Bart., at Staunton Harold in Leicestershire, for Death is the great leveller:

> In the years 1653 When all thinges sacred were throughout the nation Either demollisht or profaned Sir Robert Shirley Barronet Founded this Church Whose singular praise it is to have done the best thinges in the worst times And hoped them in the most callamitous The Righteous shall be had in everlasting remembrance.

This inscription, over the west door of the church, is not meant to be humble; Shirley, a Royalist, had done a brave deed in founding the church, and he died three years later in the Tower, aged only 27. The perfection of this prose is due to whoever finished the church and its furnishings in 1665, after the Restoration; its bluntness – 'the best thinges in the worst times' – originates in righteous wrath at the iconoclasm and vandalism of the usurpers, as well as at their regicide.

8   The Seventeenth Century: Milton

GEORGE HERBERT (1593–1633), a priest for only his last three years, and Rector of Bemerton in Wiltshire, also produced his great spiritual poetry late in life. I choose as an example of his style his sonnet *Christmas*; and I leave the original spelling for no better reason than to show how 'modern' it is, save for a couple of apostrophes where we have not really improved the system:

> All after pleasures as I rid one day,
>   My horse and I, both tir'd, bodie and minde,
> With full crie of affections, quite astray;
>   I took up in the next inne I could finde.
>
> There when I came, whom found I but my deare,
>   My dearest Lord, expecting till the grief
> Of pleasures brought me to him, readie there
>   To be all passengers most sweet relief?
>
> O Thou, whose glorious, yet contracted light,
>   Wrapt in nights mantle, stole into a manger;
> Since my dark soul and brutish is thy right,
>   To Man of all beasts be not thou a stranger:
>
> Furnish and deck my soul, that thou mayst have
> A better lodging, then a rack, or grave.

Final -*e* is of virtually no significance here; it is not pronounced, and has no grammatical function. Herbert found it necessary to distinguish the monosyllabic *tired*, which we still have, from a feasible *tirèd*, so he inserted an apostrophe; we now need one at the end (quite unjustifiably – what can it stand for *there*?) of the possessive plural *passengers* and in the possessive singular *nights*. As we saw in the opening chapter, our convention here makes no sense, since the subject-and-object plural was once *nightes* every bit as much as the genitive singular, so both should have ' or neither should. In the case of emphasising that *wrapped* has only one syllable, Herbert had handy the 'voiceless' -*t* which expresses its sound perfectly. But whatever the spelling, these inflected forms are ours also, and offer no snags.

However, there is one glaring error, to our taste: the past tense *rid*. In Old English, the infinitive, past singular, past plural, and past participle were *rīdan*, *rād*, *ridon*, *riden*, which ideally evolve in Middle English as *rīden*, *rōd*, *ridden*, *ridden*; with *us*, the past singular has swamped the past plural, but *here* the last two parts have swamped the past singular. One other anomaly may impress the reader as traditional, right, and proper: (*so*) *that thou mayst have*; but against its Old English background the subjunctive *mayst* is very wrong – the first known form was *mæge*, which would and did develop properly into *may*, but *mayst* looks more Biblical. And *whom* is of course 'wrong', since Old English *hwām* is dative.

How central, then, this great poem is to our study! – the old inflexional system virtually destroyed, a couple of grammatical subtleties disguised, and otherwise the dating revealed by the order of words and the semantic milestones that some words were still sitting on. *There when I came* is in a Latin order, *found I* is in that delightfully sensible order that the verb *do/did* has killed, *readie* 'dangles' between *me* and *him*, *dark soul and brutish* is in an Italian arrangement that we shall see in Milton, *be not* has also been destroyed by the idiom with *do*, and the two commas in the last line suggest a way of hearing the flow of words less peremptorily than is our custom. The semantic changes are considerable: not just in those words where we understand but would not imitate, as in the initial *All*, but in strongly operative words. So *full crie of affections* is a regular 'huntsman's chase of passions or lusts'; we no longer *take up* (but 'put up') at an inn; *expecting* needs an object, except in the euphemism 'She's expecting'; *passengers* now travel in a conveyance by land, sea, or air – here they are 'travellers'; *deck* is 'decorate'; *then* often doubled for *than* (and in Middle English often *vice versa*); and a *rack* is a slatted manger, not the instrument of torture.

It is likely and reasonable that I shall spend more pages on JOHN MILTON (1608–1674) than on any other writer: he presents difficulties, and some phrasing that now seems bizarre; he was a brilliant Latinist and Grecist, and wistfully coveted the idioms that he found in the Classics; he was a much greater formal scholar than Shakespeare, but not to the stifling of his imagination – rather, he sought over a wide range of scholarly topics for a vocabulary, and a placing of it, that would produce the absolute *mot juste*. He would have considered this to be his responsibility and his imperative duty; it was all very well for Shakespeare (as he saw him in *L'Allegro*) to be sweet, and the child of Fancy, warbling native wood-notes, but the map of Milton's poetry was intended to be universal, the harrowing and heartening story of God's behaviour towards Man, so the grammar of the time – as simple as ours – and the unregulated vocabulary were, to his austere taste, just not adequate.

His linguistic experiments are interesting partly in their spelling conventions, which can be no concern of this book; but 'experiments' wrongly suggests, perhaps, that the product is tentative, though it is really authoritative even when slightly ludicrous and inflated. *Paradise Lost*, the great climax of his spiritual warfare, must be used to exhibit the means of his expression and to test its success; and I think it fairest to start with a low-key speech, offering few anomalies or puzzles, in which the Father, 'without cloud, serene', mildly addresses the Son and states the consequences of the Fall (XI 57–71):

> I at first with two fair gifts
> Created him endowed – with Happiness
> And Immortality; that fondly lost,
> This other served but to eternize woe,
> Till I provided Death: so Death becomes
> His final remedy, and after life
> Tried in sharp tribulation, and refined
> By faith and faithful works, to second life,
> Waked in the renovation of the just,
> Resigns him up with Heaven and Earth renewed.
> But let us call to synod all the Blest
> Through Heaven's wide bounds; from them I will not hide
> My judgements – how with Mankind I proceed,
> As how with peccant Angels late they saw,
> And in their state, though firm, stood more confirmed.

Little evades us here – and almost nothing occasioned by the grammar or syntax. In the first line, innocuous-looking words must be read with caution: 'at the first' is the present connotation of *at first*, which otherwise looks as if God made another Creation later, and *fair* of course does not mean 'blond' or 'equitable' or 'mediocre', but a vaguer attribute like good (just as the worst mediaeval writers used it as we use 'nice'). The phrase *that fondly lost* pretends to share the force of a Latin ablative absolute; I shall return to this nostalgic idiom later, but meanwhile remember that we still use it in *during the strike* and *pending the result*, which mean 'while the strike lasts / lasted' and 'while the result is / was impending'. In the fourth line, *but* = 'only' (and the line will be broken-backed unless we stress the second syllable of *eternize*). We no longer like *Waked*, preferring *woke* for the past tense and taking refuge in forms of the verbs *waken* and *awake* for other parts. *Mankind* is strangely stressed on its first syllable, *peccant* has now lost its savour for us, and *late* for the adverb *lately* sounds illiterate. But let us proceed to a much more weird and gorgeous passage from the same epic (IX 780–794):

> So saying, her rash hand in evil hour
> Forth-reaching to the fruit, she plucked, she eat;
> Earth felt the wound, and Nature from her seat,
> Sighing through all her works, gave signs of woe
> That all was lost. Back to the thicket slunk
> The guilty Serpent, and well might, for Eve,
> Intent now wholly on her taste, naught else
> Regarded; such delight till then, as seemed,
> In fruit she never tasted, whether true,
> Or fancied so through expectation high
> Of knowledge; nor was Godhead from her thought.
> Greedily she engorged without restraint,
> And knew not eating death. Satiate at length,
> And heightened as with wine, jocund and boon,
> Thus to herself she pleasingly began:

Much of this sounds strange to us now; contorted, contrived, obsolete. Some of it would have sounded strange to Milton's readers. The subject, desperately serious, was the most mortal event in the world's history, the fall from grace and the onset of death, and it would one day be balanced by the most vital event of all, Christ's incarnation; but for this immense scene Milton chooses a style pedantic, exquisite,

Latinate, with one astonishing Grecism, and with a heavy-handed threat of anti-feminism to come. Thus we do, at least, by contrast hear the pure scream of 'Earth felt the wound'; but the ugly wit of Eve's guzzling, her not noticing the serpent's sneaky exit, and her getting big ideas, might be found tactless by people who see sin and death through human, rather than theologians', eyes.

The one real oddity is the Grecism 'knew not eating death', which has never had a place in English syntax; it hardly got a foothold in Latin syntax, though Catullus used it once and we were carefully taught the notorious instance in Virgil (*Aeneid*, II 377), *sensit medios delapsus in hostes*, 'he felt having fallen amid enemies', where the use of the past participle in the nominative case was altogether freakish. In the Latin manner, Milton pushes verbs to the ends of their sentences (*plucked, eat, Regarded, tasted, began*); *seemed* loses its *it* – no pronoun, after all, would be needed in Latin; and he pretends that *Satiate* is a past participle because it is straight from Latin *-atus* (or the supine *-atum*), whereas we make all these *-ate* verbal forms into infinitives or present stems, and the past participle needs a final *-d* – estate agents are still using this trick, so 'The property is situate in a prestige area of the Downs'.

In the midst of all this formality, it is surprising to find Milton getting his English grammar 'wrong'; *eat* is now present only, not past, but how the past tense still troubles us! – our regionalism is given away by whether we say *et* or (rhyming with *mate*) *ate*; and *slunk* sounds as wrong as the current solecisms 'We drunk the pub dry' and 'We sung in the choir' (for *drank, sang*). Milton, of course, is not 'wrong' here at all; Pepys went on using *eat* for the past, and dictionaries still allow it; and this *slunk* belongs to a time of transition from what had been Old English *slanc* to the use, even in the singular, of the plural stem *slunc-*. I do not like this kind of blurring; it brings the clear-cut verb *drink–drank–drunk* perilously nearer to the foggy forms of *cut–cut–cut*, and the like, but obviously Milton was neither ignorant of the current use nor deliberately varying it here.

There remains that unconvincing phrase 'jocund and boon'; even Wordsworth saw jocund daffodils, but we reject *boon* even when we are told that it's only French *bon* and that it still survives in 'boon companion'. And so, with the uneasy phrase which depends entirely on its order (since you can't just begin pleasingly to yourself), Milton launches out into a speech of Eve's which is in slightly less abnormal wording.

I have dwelt long on this exceptional passage; we could excuse it by pointing out that the circumstances which it relates were exceptional – indeed, unique. Milton's quirks rarely occur in such density, but they are always lurking. A well-known pair are in the adjacent lines IV 323–4 of *Paradise Lost*:

> Adam, the goodliest man of men since born
> His sons; the fairest of her daughters Eve.

This is illogical – one cannot be in the number of one's sons or daughters – but it was no newcomer in English poetry; in *Sir Gawain and the Green Knight*, the lady of the mysterious castle 'was the loveliest in skin, flesh, face, proportion, colour and qualities, of all others' (ll. 943–4) – and hard on this comes another 'mistake', the statement that 'if the young one was fresh, the other was withered' (l. 951), where in fact the truth of the main clause in no way depends on the truth of the *if*-clause: it is an 'improper *if*'. The easier Latinisms are acceptable enough, even the numerous changes of speaker as in 'To whom our Saviour sagely thus replied' (*Paradise Regained*, IV 285), which reproduces the introductory *Quo*, but they will soon turn sour, since the education of the highly literate is no longer uniformly classical; an Italianism like 'th' upright heart and pure' (*Paradise Lost*, I 18), adjective, noun, and adjective, is too easy to irritate us. But despite Milton's tributes to Latin as a guide and discipline in his poetic idiom, his painfully sincere personal utterances can work without it; brief, meant and straightforward, the sonnet *On His Blindness* now needs few glosses:

> When I consider how my light is spent,
>   Ere half my days in this dark world and wide,
>   And that one talent which is death to hide
> Lodged with me useless, though my soul more bent
> To serve therewith my Maker, and present
>   My true account, lest He returning chide;
>   'Doth God exact day-labour, light denied?'
> I fondly ask; but Patience, to prevent
>   That murmur, soon replies, 'God doth not need
>   Either man's work or His own gifts. Who best
>   Bear his mild yoke, they serve Him best: His state

Is kingly: thousands at His bidding speed,
  And post o'er land and ocean without rest;
    They also serve who only stand and wait.

To annotate this in due order, I would simply point out that *Ere* was still an alternative for *before*; *dark world and wide* most resembles Italian; *talent* is a handsome pun all ready for Milton in Christ's parable, the word meaning both a large sum of money and a natural expertise; *chide* is a third person singular present subjunctive, for something that could happen but could be guarded against, whereas *Doth* shows the former *-th* of the third person singular present indicative (and of course *-s* now dully seeks to cover both these forms); *light denied* is a pale reflection of a Latin ablative absolute, 'light-having-been-denied', but it was always risky to pretend that *we* had ablative nouns as well; *fondly* means 'foolishly' – just as 'I'm fond of her' means 'I'm silly about her'; *Who* is a Latinism for 'He who'.

It would not be right to cease from mention of Milton without using a little of his prose, if only as an antidote to his poetic diction, which no one truly inherited – though he had centuries of pious imitators. His tract on censorship, *Areopagitica*, was published in 1644, twenty-three years before *Paradise Lost*, and reveals a blithe and witty conversational style, composed yet in its asides staccato, nicely varied in its native and Romance vocabulary. I have chosen here to keep the original spelling, which – in *bin* and *servil* especially – imparts something of the poet's speaking voice:

> . . . And lest some should perswade ye, Lords and Commons, that these arguments of lerned men . . . are meer flourishes, and not reall, I could recount what I have seen and heard in other Countries, where this kind of inquisition tyrannizes; when I have sat among their lerned men, – for that honor I had, – and bin counted happy to be born in such a place of *Philosophic* freedom, as they suppos'd England was, while themselves did nothing but bemoan the servil condition into which lerning amongst them was brought; that this was it which had dampt the glory of Italian wits; that nothing had bin there writt'n now these many years but flattery and fustian.

A few surprising things happen; *ye* as the object of a verb (instead of *you*) is a mistake which we saw Shakespeare making in *Henry VIII*, and we would hardly expect Milton, steeped in the many *ye* and *you* forms of the Bible, and himself properly trained in grammar, to make this blunder – but the word was growing antiquated. The anglicised misspelling of *persuade*, with a *w* unheard-of in the Latin alphabet, grates on me and ought to have offended him. We now associate *honor* with Latin if we have studied 'the tongues', but with Noah Webster's nit-picking when we deplore the futile little modifications which he and other amateurs imposed on American English – *honor* no more saying 'onr' than *honour* does. Milton is insisting on the mere two syllables of *suppos'd* with that apostrophe, but *themselves*, as if it were *ipsi* and needed no pronoun, and the postfixed verb *was brought*, hanker after Latin. And whereas *dampt* is a very realistic spelling of the past participle of a verb with a voiceless stop ending its stem, *writt'n* is easily pronounceable only because its *n* elides with the following *n* in *now*; (but on this see Alan Ward, 'Milton's Spellings Again', in *Five Hundred Years of Words and Sounds for E. J. Dobson* (Cambridge: D. S. Brewer, 1983), pp. 157–64). *Wits* and *fustian* may puzzle us without a good dictionary, but they ring with colloquial frankness here. *Philosophic* and similar suffixed words are now causing endless trouble; we hesitate over *dialect* (substantive and adjective), *dialectal*, *dialectic*, *dialectical* (all adjectives in origin, though who has not heard of 'Marxist dialectic'?), and *-ic* and other suffixes are a prey to this over-elaboration. Legislation is needed, of the type that quite unhistorically laid it down that *-itis* is for inflammations.

9 Informal English: Aubrey

Almost all the texts presented in this book have been subjected to polish by their authors (often men of great learning), their authors' friends and editors, and subsequent rescuers of their manuscripts. So it is right to use a text which has been caught with its hair down, in the hope that it represents more faithfully than most the actual thoughts and intonations of the writer. JOHN AUBREY (1626–1697) left in manuscript, and sometimes in a kind of shorthand, 426 *Minutes of Lives*, customarily called the *Brief Lives*; the most familiar edition is of 134 of these, by O. L. Dick (Harmondsworth: Penguin, 1972). As bestowed on posterity, *The Lives* are often scruffy, and have to be edited by conflation, omission, and attempts to fill in all his gaps. But they are well adapted to our special purpose, and the scandalous, sometimes pithy and sometimes verbose, speaking voice comes clearly through to us. One of his more famous subjects, Francis Bacon,

> was wont to say to his servant Hunt (who was a notable thrifty man and loved this World and the only servant he had that he could never get to become bound for him) *The World was made for man, Hunt, and not man for the World* . . . [my lacuna] None of his servaunts durst appeare before him without Spanish leather bootes; for he would smelle the neates leather, which offended him. The East India Merchants presented his Lordship with a Cabinet of Jewells, which his Page, Mr Cockaine, received and deceived his Lord . . . His Lordship would many times have Musique in the next roome where he meditated.

As the jottings of a man who died in 1697, this passage has an old-fashioned feel. What Aubrey knew of the venerable history of *wont*, the past participle that goes right back to the Old English verb *wunian*, is impossible to say, but in our ignorance we might suppose him wrong in saying *notable thrifty* instead of the adverb *notably*; *durst* should surprise no one in Bristol, where it is still the vigorous past tense (*and* the conditional) of *dare*; but *neates leather* looks back, for those of us who know *Julius Caesar*, to the whimsical cobbler in the first scene, and forward to our old-fashioned nostrum, neat's-foot oil. The neighbourhood of *received* and *deceived* suggests the lack of polish on the book, and in the ambiguity of Bacon's having music *in the next roome where he meditated* we see the overhasty style that conceals the more practical *to where*.

Thomas Bushell 'had the strangest bewitching way to drawe-in people . . . into his projects that ever I heard of. His tongue was a Charme, and drewe in so many . . .'. Here Aubrey hits on a way to distinguish the infinitive of a 'verb + adverb' verb, by hyphenating them, but hesitates to do the same with the past tense. When sufficiently moved by a great subject, Aubrey's general style grows strong and handsome; so the heroic Royalist general, Charles Cavendish, killed at Gainsborough when he was 23, is given this encomium:

> An high Extraction to some persons is like the Dropsie, the greatnesse of the man is his disease, and renders him unwieldie: but here is a Person of great Extract free from the swelling of Greatness, as brisk and active as the lightest Horseman that fought under him. In some parts of India, they tell us, that a Nobleman accounts himselfe polluted if a Plebeian touch him; but here is a person of that rank who used the same familiaritie and frankness amongst the meanest of his Souldiers, the poorest miner, and amongst his equalls; and by stooping so low, he rose the higher in the common account, and was valued accordingly as a Prince, and a Great one.

An before an aspirated *h* is not now standard use; nor is *the* before the name of a complaint like dropsy. *Extract* as a noun is swamped by medical and culinary terms such as *malt extract*. In *they tell us, that*, we would now suppress the comma or the *that*; *touch* is subjunctive after *if*.

Aubrey relished people who did the unexpected in their exalted stations; the free-and-easy Richard Corbet, Bishop of Oxford and Norwich, was one such:

One time, as he was Confirming, the country-people pressing in to see the Ceremonie [the absolute construction again], sayd he, *Beare off there, or I'le* [not an historical spelling] *confirm yee* [Wolsey's mistake for *you*] *with my Staffe*. Another time, being to [= *having to, being about to*] lay his hand on the head of a man very bald [a rare, but emphatic, word-order], he turns [still our anecdotal present tense] to his chaplaine, Lushington, and sayd [back to the past], *Some Dust, Lushington* (to keepe his hand from slipping). There was a man with a great venerable Beard: sayd the Bishop, *You, behind the Beard*.

Amid so much anecdotage, Aubrey still finds time for descriptive touches: Stourhead (in the *Life* of William Herbert) is 'a most parkely ground and Romancy pleasant place: heretofore all horrid, and woody', and the five adjectives – especially with that *frisson* of enjoyable horror – still convey the spirit of this National Trust property, though there are now joyous rhododendrons. His unpolished, even unplanned, sentences do not help the reader: the father of Sir John Denham built at Egham 'a house very convenient, not great, but pretty, and pleasantly scituated, and in which his son, Sir John (though he had better seates) did take most delight in' – where the clause beginning 'and in which' should be just 'in which', and the final 'in' is a mere repetition. Or a harmless change of construction will slightly unhinge a sentence: John Milton's young wife 'oftimes heard his Nephews beaten and cry' (part participle and infinitive, where the present participle *crying* would be a better parallel). If there is a popular form of an irregular verb, he is happy to produce it, and Sir Thomas Morgan 'seek't his fortune (as a soldier)', though *we* still retain *sought*. Almost, at times, he appears to be writing with a forced monosyllabic bareness, and in this sentence we miss the 'if' of a true conditional clause and the 'would have' of a true past conditional statement: Sir William Petty 'is of Mr Hobbes his [the old error for *Hobbes's*] mind, that had he read much, as some men have, he had not known so much as he does'. We have spent rather long over one who might not be commonly granted a place in literature, but he speaks to us straight, and – with no reason to parade words or conceal them – he must be a fair index of the contemporary language of broadminded wits and gentlemen. His report of the imperfect Edmund Waller, the turncoat poet, relies on his subject's direct speech as well as his own comment:

When he was a brisque young sparke, and first studyed Poetry [*study* has not yet made the quiet change to -*i*- in the past]; me thought [still the old *thinken* 'to seem'], sayd he, I never sawe a good copie of English verses; they want [= 'lack'] smoothness; then I began to essay [= 'try' – a pupil's essay is only a trial-piece]. I have severall times heard him say that he cannot versify when he will [= 'wants to']: but when the Fitt comes upon him, he does it easily.

10 The Eighteenth Century: Gothic Revival English

The steady, tasteful decency of JOSEPH ADDISON (1672–1719), son of a Dean of Lichfield and husband of a Countess of Warwick, promises hymns more educated than ecstatic, but though few of us could recite from memory any parts of the respectable essays that form his journalism, he is still remembered for some hymns. One, beginning *The spacious firmament on high* and graced with several good tunes, is apparently still a great favourite with Freemasons; it states with poise a paradox that not every Christian finds instructive – that the heavenly bodies make a silent music of praise – and it could hardly be more lucidly expressed. We expect the dignity of *Doth* and *taketh*, and get *Does* and *takes*; *whilst* (a slovenly form of older *whiles*) is a concession to fine writing; two hard words occur – *frame* meaning 'construction' and *Original* for something like 'Originator/Creator'; one archaism breaks the modern course of the syntax, 'nor real voice nor sound', where one would now say *neither* for the first *nor*, but it is good to see the disyllable *real* in these days when too many people reply to information with 'Oh, reely?'

But his hymn translating the 23rd Psalm and beginning 'The Lord my pasture shall prepare' neither adds anything useful to the original nor reproduces its lovely candour and simplicity. It appeared in *The Spectator* for 26 July 1712 (No. 441), and the three stanzas after the first are a rather gingerly exercise in heightening the original; the oddities are such that my mother assured me that one of her Sunday School pupils, bemused by the rhymes on *prepare* and *supply* at the beginning, recited the first two lines as

69

'The Lord my pasture shall supply,
And feed me with a shepherd's pie [*read* 'care']'.

When in the sultry glebe I faint,
Or on the thirsty mountain pant;
To fertile vales and dewy meads,
My weary wand'ring steps he leads;
Where peaceful rivers soft and slow,
Amid the verdant landskip flow.

Tho' in the paths of death I tread,
With gloomy horrors over-spread;
My steadfast heart shall fear no ill,
For thou, O Lord, art with me still;
Thy friendly crook shall give me aid,
And guide me through the dreadful shade.

Tho' in a bare and rugged way,
Through devious lonely wilds I stray,
Thy bounty shall my pains beguile:
The barren wilderness shall smile
With sudden greens and herbage crown'd.
And streams shall murmur all around.

Yet almost none of the antiquarianism is caused by a superseded grammar. It is the diction that plays the tedious (or amusing) tricks: *glebe* is (and was chiefly then) the technical term for the 'parson's piece', the 'church land', though its original, Latin *gleba*, was broader – 'clod, earth, soil'; *faint* is now 'pass out', and for the meaning here intended we need *feel faint*; *mead*, though still gracing the name of Bristol's chief station, Temple Meads ('meadows belonging to the Knights Templars'), has always been an ambiguous phoneme, since it also meant 'reward' (in another spelling) and a potent 'drink made with honey'; *ill* (a little flavoured by Addison's time) has been replaced by 'evil' – and a good thing, too, since it was already adjective and adverb (*ill advised*) as well as noun; *shade* is rather nice on a sultry day, and its menace must now be conveyed by *shadow*; the *sudden greens* suggest an onset of cabbages, and I am told that the phrase *friendly crook* diverts worshippers in prison chapels. Five other departures from the norm further complicate this already loaded hymn. Since mountains cannot feel thirst, the second line has a 'transferred epithet', in as much as the mountains *induce* the thirst in humans; *landskip* is nearer to the Dutch word from which we borrowed it; *Tho'* was by Addison's time an affected spelling, since no one would have pronounced *Though* differently; who or what is 'over-spread'? – the poet (with horrors), the paths (with horrors), or the horrors (spread all over the place)? – because this is a bad 'dangling participle'; and what shall beguile what? – only the fool would read this as 'my pains shall beguile Thy bounty', but in the absence of any clear 'cases' this reading is grammatically possible.

It is handy to quote a writer who can announce for us the dawn of each new century, so at the risk of being unfair to ALEXANDER POPE (1688–1744) by using something which he wrote at sixteen, in 1704, I have chosen a rather pink-and-white passage from *Summer: The Second Pastoral* (lines 41–58). There is no trace yet of the later bitterness staunched by discipline, or of the cruel bad manners polished by words that are without vulgarity.

> He said; Alexis, take this pipe, the same
> That taught the groves my Rosalinda's name:
> But now the reeds shall hang on yonder tree,
> For ever silent, since despis'd by thee.
> Oh! were I made by some transforming pow'r
> The captive bird that sings within thy bow'r!
> Then might my voice thy list'ning ears employ,
> And I those kisses he receives, enjoy.
>   And yet my numbers please the rural throng,
> Rough Satyrs dance, and Pan applauds the song:
> The Nymphs, forsaking ev'ry cave and spring,
> Their early fruit, and milk-white turtles bring;
> Each am'rous nymph prefers her gifts in vain,
> On you their gifts are all bestow'd again.
> For you the swains the fairest flow'rs design,
> And in one garland all their beauties join;
> Accept the wreath which you deserve alone,
> In whom all beauties are compris'd in one.

Shakespeare's Rosalind had an Arden more real than this, and Orlando surely had a better tan than this wan lover. Behind *these* swains and nymphs, however, lie the pastoral youth (one cannot call them 'folk') of Greek and Latin poetry, and the vocabulary – not the inflexional system – is Pope's way of presenting the speech of these pretty people; he was growing up into a stunted little fellow, and there is a deadly pathos in this picture of Arcadia. The heavy rhyme announced by *the same* is saying no more than *the one*, *the same one*, or just *which*; never in any letter, however formal, give way to the once-admired 'thanks for same'; *groves* are just woods, not avenues; *bow'r* is not Classical but Old English, and it appears to have extricated itself from the former meaning of 'women's sleeping-quarters, bedroom', and modestly become 'chamber' or even 'pergola, arbour'; *numbers* are 'tunes, songs, poems', and it is vital to realise that the *turtles* are not those great plated creatures but white turtle-doves; *prefers* now is 'shows a preference for', but here it means 'proffers'; since the gifts are being handed on to someone else, *again* here means 'in turn'; and *swains*, which had had a martial ring loudest in the belligerent King Sweyn, is gentle here, and they are wreathing the prettiest (not the most blond, equitable, or mediocre) flowers. This sorted out, we may feel that Pope is one of *us*, until we see the other modifications which he feels obliged to make; at 16, it is his ear – rather than long training in the craft – that suggested these. In an inhabited landscape as delicate as one by Fragonard or Greuze, the rough *yonder* cuts the shepherds to a little nearer size, and his dislike of feminine rhymes (a couplet of 11-syllabled lines rhyming on *túm-tee* rather than *túm*) makes him carefully show *'pow'r'* and *'bow'r'* as monosyllables; but even in mid-line he decides to take this precaution – *despis'd*, *list'ning*, *am'rous*, *bestow'd* and *compris'd* are all thus cut down from three syllables to two, and so to our great surprise is *ev'ry*, which we would never now make a trisyllable. With no *e* pronounced in the *-ed* termination, we have real cause to wonder whether the inflexion had not completely turned by then into *-d/-t*. One last caution: Pope is not to blame for the present misrhyming of *design*, *join* and *alone*, *one*; currently, they were correct – in fact *alone*, *one* is a self-rhyme, since 'alone' is literally 'quite one'.

Let us look at Dr Johnson through the report of JAMES BOSWELL (1740–1795), in a style that owes much to his loved master: orderly, living, bland. Johnson has just remarked to Boswell, as they hurry along in the post-chaise, 'Life has not many things better than this';

then they make a tea-and-coffee stop at Stratford, and their next but one topic is Grainger's poem *The Sugar-Cane*.

I mentioned to him Mr Langton's having told me, that this poem, when read in manuscript at Sir Joshua Reynolds's, had made all the assembled wits burst into a laugh, when, after much blank verse pomp, the poet began a new paragraph thus:

'Now, Muse, let's sing of *rats*'.

And what increased the ridicule was, that one of the company, who slyly overlooked the reader, perceived that the word had been originally *mice*, and had been altered to *rats*, as more dignified.

This passage does not appear in the printed work, Dr Grainger, or some of his friends, it should seem, having become sensible that introducing even *rats*, in a grave poem, might be liable to banter.

The incidents happened in 1776; the wording would not have confused intelligent readers in 1976. But there are three small differences: that *become sensible* at the end could be 'become sensitive to the fact' or just 'realised'; *it should seem* is odd, as if suggesting a moral obligation for the realisation to occur to the friends; and *overlooked* goes on being an unhappy ambiguity – *ignored* or *scrutinised* (by peeping over the reader's shoulder). But notice the good and enduring example which the passage sets us! – before the verbal noun *having* in the first line, Mr Langton is shown in the possessive case (*not* 'Do you object to me smoking?'). *Reynolds's* has its correct possessive, despite all the buzzes. Perhaps Boswell is a little too careful for our tastes in applying commas after 'having told me' and 'what increased the ridicule was', where I would certainly read the latter with no pause save a slight one after 'ridicule'.

Later in the same year, having *lain* for a night at Henley (that is, 'stayed' or 'put up', as in the misinterpreted medieval lyric, 'He cam also stylle ther His moder lay'), they reached Birmingham to call on a Mr Hector.

A very stupid maid, who opened the door, told us, [again, our voices would over-ride this comma] that 'her master [nor do we put reported speech in quotation marks] was gone out [and this French-sounding, but in fact good Old English, use of *be*, not *have*, with intransitive verbs, has nearly quitted our speech]; he was gone to [*into* now sounds more familiar] the country; she could not tell when he would return'. . . . He said to her, 'My name is Johnson; tell him I called. Will you remember the name?' She answered with rustick [this -*k* was a long time dying, but is now extinct] simplicity, in the Warwickshire pronunciation, 'I don't understand you, Sir'. – 'Blockhead, (said he,) [a shaky piece of punctuation] I'll write'. I never heard the word *blockhead* applied to a woman before, though I do not see why it should not [should not *what*? – this obviously needs the addition of 'be'], when there is evident occasion for it. He, however, made another attempt to make her understand him, and roared loud [-ly!] in her ear, 'Johnson', and then she catched the sound [*catch* is a French word, and the irregular 'caught' is a falsification of its history; this well excuses the unattractive 'catched'].

Boswell is obviously a bit worried about *blockhead*; he quotes in support of it an honest carpenter who told a parson's wife that she was a *scoundrel* for underpaying him; in 1752, he reports Johnson as calling some young ladies 'a set of wretched un-idea'd girls', where I would probably spell it out as *unideaed*, however strange it looked. This frankness about Johnson's rather unchivalrous treatment of girls suggests more strongly than ever that Boswell was not choosing the best remarks but was reporting accurately, that when Johnson said of his pet cat, 'But Hodge shan't be shot: no, no, Hodge shall not be shot', we may presume a difference of emphasis between 'shan't' and 'shall not'. If anyone offers the objection that Johnson talks in an epistolary style, we can answer that he also writes letters in a speaking voice, as in one written to Boswell on the first day of 1775, and reproduced in *The Life of Samuel Johnson, D.D.*:

Dear Sir,

I long to hear how you like the book; it is, I think, much liked here. But Macpherson is very furious; can you give me any more intelligence about him, or his Fingal? Do what you can, and do it quickly. Is Lord Hailes on our side? [We might, in fact, find 'much liked' too informal; 'very furious' would not now be used, though there is no saying why; 'intelligence' is neither braininess nor secret strategic information, but just 'news', here required about Macpherson's 'Ossian' spoof].

Pray let me know what I owed you when I left you, that I may send it to you. [I have never heard 'Pray' used thus, seriously, the nearest being a deprecating use in Bletchley, 'Oh, pray!' And the omission of 'so' before 'that' in a purpose clause belongs now only to hymnody].

I am going to write about the Americans. If you have picked up any hints among your lawyers, who are great masters of the law of nations, or if your own mind suggest [present subjunctive without -*s*] any thing [now one word], let me know. But mum [now used only dependently, as in 'mum's the word' or 'keep mum'], it is a secret. . . .

Langton is here; we are all that ever we were [friends] . . .

Reynolds has taken too much to strong liquour . . .

As you love verses, I will send you a few which I made upon [the subject, not the soil, of] Inchkenneth . . . [Lord Hailes] must promise not to let them be copied again, nor [we say 'or'!] to shew [still the elegant spelling] them as mine . . .

Between late-mediaeval balladry, the story of the king and the beggar-maid as known to Shakespeare in *Romeo and Juliet* (II i 14), Richard Johnson's printing of the story in his *Crown Garland of Goulden Roses* (1612), and the version issued by THOMAS PERCY (1729–1811), Bishop of Dromore, many 'improvements' may have occurred; he says that he has 'corrected' Johnson from another copy. I am using here the four-volume 1823 edition (the sixth) of his *Reliques of Ancient English Poetry*, in which time, and the 'improvements' which taste and scholarship thought fit, had imposed on an eager reading public in 1765 a mighty strange version of the older form of English. At I 315 occurs 'King Cophetua and the Beggar-Maid':

I read that once in Affrica
  A princely wight did raine,
Who had to name Cophetua,
  As poets they did faine:
From natures lawes he did decline,
For sure he was not of my mind,
He cared not for women-kinde,
  But did them all disdaine.
But, marke, what hapened on a day,
As he out of his window lay,
He saw a beggar all in grey,
  The which did cause his paine.

The blinded boy, that shootes so trim,
  From heaven downe did hie;
He drew a dart and shot at him,
  In place where he did lye:
Which soone did pierse him to the quicke,
And when he felt the arrow pricke,
Which in his tender heart did sticke,
  He looketh as he would dye.

The jog-trot rhythm, the many line-fillers (*did* nine times, *poets they*, *The which, place where*), and the generally trivial attitude, do not reflect the state of early narrative poetry, and in so edited an idiom it is hard to trust even those words that have an archaic ring – *wight, faine, marke, trim, hie*. In the first line, *read* has long been a nuisance, since it is intrinsically neither present (and pronounced 'reed') nor past (and pronounced 'red'); I have a little idiosyncrasy of writing these two with a breve or a macron above them, as in Classical scansion. The spelling *poets* at once gives the lie to the spelling *lawes*, which certainly can't have two syllables, whereas *cared* has to have two – though this in turn is no guide to *hapened*, where the second *-e* must be elided. The grammar has its inconsistency, too; Cupid in the present tense *shootes*, where the *s* is the modern form, but in the last line the king *looketh* in the good old way. The addition of final *-e* to so many words, or the pretence that it is a genuine relic, comes to no harm on the infinitives *raine, faine, disdaine, pricke, sticke*, or the dative noun *quicke* after a preposition – but why not then on *mind, day, window, grey, heaven, heart*, which are variously after *of, on, of, in, from, in*? Of *marke* it should just be added that it clings on in two phrases – 'mark my words' and the Church's 'read, mark, learn'.

It is the sheer addition of final *-e* indiscriminately to words, to give them a mediaeval look, which betrays the fake Middle English of THOMAS CHATTERTON (1752–1770); his harmless forgeries ran from the summer of 1768 to the spring of 1769, when he was 15–16, and despite his peeps at a few specimens of an older English, his mediaeval linguistics depend on capricious spellings, some invented words, the spirit of Spenser, some genuine dictionary forms, and that ubiquitous final *-e*, often in contexts where Middle English would never have borne it. All this has nothing to do with the sharpness of his vision or the swell and panache of his rhythms, but it will be seen at once that the diction is seventeenth-century or somewhat archaic English, *plus* pom-poms. It took in Horace Walpole, but not his less dilettante friend Thomas Gray. In his remarkable tragedy *Ælla*, begun in December 1768, and not performed until 1970, Chatterton allotted speeches which, stripped of their trimmings, have a grave eloquence; the hero is preparing to resist the Danes (*Ælla*, ll. 706ff.):

> Now havynge done oure mattynes and oure vowes,
>   Lette us for the intended fyghte be boune,
>   And everyche champyone potte the joyous crowne
> Of certane masterschyppe upon hys glestreynge browes.

> As for mie harte, I owne ytt ys, as ere
>   Itte has beene ynne the sommer-sheene of fate,
> Unknowen to the ugsomme gratche of fere;
>   Mie blodde embollen, wythe masterie elate,
>   Boyles ynne mie veynes, and rolles ynn rapyd state,
>   Impatyente forr to mete the persante stele,
>   And telle the worlde, thatte Ælla dyed as greate
>   As anie knyghte who foughte for Englondes weale.
>   Friends, kynne, and soldyerres, ynne blacke
>   armore drere,
>   Mie actyons ymytate, mie presente redynge
>   here.

The exercise of restoring this to its real language is easy; but when it is done, we realise that there subsists a wonderful, and not always fortuitous, language of heroic and archaic ideals: *sommer* happens to be a good Middle English form (*somer* is better), with *summer* given an *o* to make it easier to read next to the other 'minim' letter *m*; how have we managed without *ugsom*? – and who need be offended by a past participle as telling as *embollen*? Some of Chatterton's forms are flatly ignorant: 'so haveth I' was never right in any period or dialect, his rhymes are often modern, his syllable-counting makes *-tion* into one syllable instead of the traditional two; but even when he invents a form like *dhey* 'they', it announces its sound and even *looks* authentic.

11 The Nineteenth Century: 'language really used by men'

It would be wrong to judge the realism of MARIA EDGEWORTH (1767–1849) from the genteel parlour-talk and posturing which I am about to quote; she was active in the work of education, especially for females, modifying the principles of Rousseau's *Émile*, and she worked hard for victims of the Irish famine in 1846. But her novels can sound stuffy and privileged, with slothful conversations that never infringe propriety. This passage is from Chapter V of *Patronage* (1814):

> 'Some of these novels are sad trash – I hope Mr Godfrey Percy will not judge of my taste by them: that would be condemning me for the crime of my bookseller, who will send us down everything new that comes out'. Godfrey disclaimed the idea of condemning or blaming Miss Hauton's taste: 'he could not,' he said, 'be so presumptuous, so impertinent.' 'So then,' said she, 'Mr Godfrey Percy is like all the rest of his sex, and I must not expect to hear the truth from him ... I would, however, rather have him speak severely than think hardly of me.' 'He has no right to speak, and certainly no inclination to think hardly of Miss Hauton,' replied Godfrey gravely, but with an emotion which he in vain endeavoured to suppress. To change the conversation, he asked her opinion about a figure in the print. She took out her glass, and stooped to look.

With all the time in the world, Miss Hauton prefers *judge of* to *judge*, and can think out nice antitheses like *speak severely . . . think hardly*. The

78

author, meanwhile, is making everything distractingly involved by putting the indirect speech into quotation marks. What is said is so stately, on the smallest issues, that it is a surprise to hear the lady use the slack phrase *sad trash*, where *sad* bears no relation to grief (our equivalent would be something like 'miserable, wretched, rotten, poor'), and where *trash* reminds us most strongly of an American trash-can. Her idiom *will send* is an expression of the present, especially of an action customary and repeated. The lady withholds from the swain the pronoun 'you'; he is left in the third person, and she is kept remote by him in the same way, but out of a kind of awe. Suddenly a novelettish style takes over with a dangerous surge of passion which (*To change the conversation*) he ruthlessly curbs; but that *emotion which he in vain endeavoured to suppress* has told on him, and the safe refuge is a picture, whereat she takes out her *glass*, an eye-glass not a tumbler, and bends over to look, not *stooped* in the sense of 'deigned'.

In the high Middle Ages one wrote in the vernacular compulsively, with no plan of founding a school of writers; true, alliterative poets had a specialised (or you might call it limited) workshop training, but Chaucer is the first we know to have founded a circle. From Spenser on, we have more truly imitated, and remembered our masters even if it means aping their grammar and falsifying our own. It is sometimes assumed that the test of a great creative mind is whether a writer can be parodied, in which case he is imitable and falls short; Hopkins can be parodied well enough to bluff the enthusiast – but who has dared, or managed, to produce convincing Shakespeare, or the intensity and reserve of Eliot – or at least, the Eliot of *The Waste Land* or *Four Quartets*? After the long career of Miltonic 'blank', the excellent example of Dryden and Pope's couplets, and the timid but strengthening murmurs of the pre-Romantics, the deliberately fresh start at the close of the 1700s was made by WILLIAM WORDSWORTH (1770–1850) in *Lyrical Ballads* (1798), with a somewhat dissimilar contribution by Coleridge. In the 1800 preface, Wordsworth says that he was trying to

choose incidents and situations from common life, and to relate or describe them, throughout, as far as was possible in a selection of language really used by men, and, at the same time, to throw over

them a certain colouring of imagination, whereby ordinary things
should be presented to the mind in an unusual aspect. Humble and
rustic life was generally chosen. . . . The language . . . of these men
has been adopted (purified indeed from what appear to be its real
defects, from all lasting and rational causes of dislike or disgust)
because such men hourly communicate with the best objects from
which the best part of language is originally derived. . . . Such a
language, arising out of repeated experience and regular feelings, is
a more permanent, and a far more philosophical language, than
that which is frequently substituted for it by Poets.

I regret that word 'philosophical' and the suggestion that Cumbrian
(and other peasant) language needed tidying-up so as to remove
disgusting and distasteful bits, and equally the suggestion that the
'best part of language' stems from a land-locked pastoral economy;
but it was a sincere endeavour. We all know the results – on the one
hand the meanness, the affected drabness, of that notorious pond:

I've measured it from side to side:
'Tis three feet long, and two feet wide;

or the abandoned first line of *We Are Seven*, which now leaves it
half-headless:

A simple Child, dear brother Jim;

or the suddenly posh 'agèd utensil' (with the accent on the first
syllable) in *Michael*, much as Coleridge's old sailor in the same volume
became an ancient mariner. Wordsworth's reaction from this simple,
and at times excessively simple, language, when it came upon him in
his desuetude, was far worse, and the child who in ?1802 had come
'trailing clouds of glory' turned by 1827 into 'A Growth from sinful
Nature's bed of weeds'.

But in all this, Wordsworth did not falsify or strain the inherited
grammar and syntax, though the vocabulary can turn quaint. The
frank and happy opening,

I wandered lonely as a cloud
That floats on high o'er vales and hills,

must have its *o'er* and its *vales*, but I actually heard 'ower' for *over* in the Vale of St John, and it is not until we reach the *jocund company* of the daffodils, or the poet's *vacant* mood on his *couch*, that the shepherds quite cease to speak. The real simplicity of Wordsworth's expression, which has endlessly refreshed us, can be seen in a number of his poems of lesser fame, such as *The Reverie of Poor Susan* (1797), where the unhappy girl is the precursor of those thousands of Victorian peasants who came to the cities to escape rural penury, and never returned:

> At the corner of Wood Street, when daylight appears,
> Hangs a Thrush that sings loud, it has sung for three years:
> Poor Susan has passed by the spot, and has heard
> In the silence of morning the song of the Bird.

(It has now become mysteriously funny to repeat a simple noun by means of its synonym. In the sarcastic *Anglicans' Alphabet* occur the lines

> E is the Eagle, sublime and absurd,
> F is the Females who polish that bird;

Hilaire Belloc on *The Python* is all the funnier because its last line is

> The Snake is living yet;

and the droll quatrain, used in wartime security propaganda, is the more effective because the owl ends by being generalised:

> A wise old Owl sat in an oak.
> The more he heard the less he spoke.
> The less he spoke the more he heard.
> Soldiers should imitate this bird.

Otherwise, the stanza, apart from the imaginative touch of making the thrush 'hang', is wonderfully normal; *loud* for 'loudly' slightly slangy, and the comma after it dividing two sentences where a semi-colon would have been more orthodox).

'Tis a note of enchantment; what ails her? She sees
A mountain ascending, a vision of trees;
Bright volumes of vapour through Lothbury glide,
And a river flows on through the vale of Cheapside.

('*Tis* is of course good rustic speech, though my experience of it is most
strongly linked with Devon; *ails* has nearly perished now, and will be a
neat word lost).

Green pastures she views in the midst of the dale,
Down which she so often has tripped with her pail;
And a single small cottage, a nest like a dove's,
The one only dwelling on earth that she loves.

(The word *tripped* now looks out of place; we flippantly see her falling
flat, bucket flying. *The one only* is prettily put, but less acceptable than
our hackneyed 'one and only').

She looks, and her heart is in heaven: but they fade,
The mist and the river, the hill and the shade:
The stream will not flow, and the hill will not rise,
And the colours have all passed away from her eyes!

There have been no sham '*d* spellings here, no fancy vocabulary, no
seeing further than a peasant's eye. The result is a record of pure
compassion for tragedy.

Gratitude to Wordsworth should often be mingled with as great a
gratitude to his sister DOROTHY WORDSWORTH (1771–1855),
whose *Journals* of 1798 and 1800–1803 show her so often to be the eyes
and even the mind behind some of his freshest and most honest
poetry. There is no 'jocund company' in her observation of those
daffodils on the shores of Ullswater; there is little punctuation, either,
but her words are poetry already:

When we were in the woods beyond Gowbarrow park we saw a few
daffodils close to the water side. We fancied that the lake had

floated the seeds ashore and that the little colony had so sprung up. But as we went along there were more and yet more and at last under the boughs of the trees, we saw that there was a long belt of them along the shore, about the breadth of a country turnpike road. I never saw daffodils so beautiful they grew among the mossy stones about and about them, some rested their heads upon these stones as on a pillow for weariness and the rest tossed and reeled and danced and seemed as if they verily laughed with the wind that blew upon them over the lake, they looked so gay ever glancing ever changing. The wind blew directly over the lake to them. There was here and there a little knot and a few stragglers a few yards higher up but they were so few as not to disturb the simplicity and unity and life of that one busy highway. We rested again and again. The Bays were stormy, and we heard the waves at different distances and in the middle of the water like the sea.

Left to himself, with this sparkling report as his guide, Wordsworth added the vacant or pensive moods felt on his couch, and calmed the waves to a dance and a sparkle; the *turnpike road* and the *busy highway*, imaginative comparisons, are dimly recalled in his *milky way*, but a slight stodginess has set in, and her breathless, headlong syntax, reflecting the perpetual flurry of the daffodils, is controlled by a formal metre. And, interestingly, her grammar is utterly ours, with not even any poetic diction save *verily*.

A poet much afflicted with pain, nausea, poverty, a wretched marriage, and the collapse of his aspirations, who can yet write in a letter that after a big meal and a sea bathe his 'triumphant tripes cataracted Niagaraishly', obviously has resources of facetiousness. SAMUEL TAYLOR COLERIDGE (1772–1834) had many influences bearing on his vocabulary and idiom: childhood in a Devon vicarage, schooldays up in London at Christ's Hospital, unprofitable years at Cambridge, voracious reading with philosophy at its core, and the formative friendship with William Wordsworth, who had those famous and stated ideas on reporting for poetry the speech of ordinary men. Lines 64–77 and 86–92 of Coleridge's *The Nightingale* (April 1798) are a pleasing concoction:

A most gentle Maid
Who dwelleth in her hospitable home
Hard by the Castle, and at latest eve,
(Even like a Lady vow'd and dedicate
To something more than nature in the grove)
Glides thro' the pathways; she knows all their
    notes,
That gentle Maid! and oft, a moment's space,
What time the moon was lost behind a cloud,
Hath heard a pause of silence: till the Moon
Emerging, hath awaken'd earth and sky
With one sensation, and those wakeful Birds
Have all burst forth with choral minstrelsy,
As if one quick and sudden Gale had swept
An hundred airy harps! . . .
Full fain it would delay me! My dear Babe,
Who, capable of no articulate sound,
Mars all things with his imitative lisp,
How he would place his hand beside his ear,
His little hand, the small forefinger up,
And bid us listen! And I deem it wise
To make him Nature's playmate.

But a grammarian could hardly treat these lines as typical of their
age; the turn of the eighteenth and nineteenth centuries finds the poet,
whose ideas were considered advanced and unorthodox, using a
ragbag of diction, which yet gets stitched up into poetry. The verb
inflexions waver, in the present tense, between third person singular
in -*eth* (always more cadenced than its supplanter) like *dwelleth, hath*
(twice), and in -*s* like *Glides, knows, Mars*. The pretence (which we
detected in Milton) that verbs in -*ate* are still Latin -*atus* participles,
and not yet infinitives at all, allows the lady to be *dedicate* instead of
dedicated; another Miltonic Latinism, as if reproducing the ablative
absolute, is *the small forefinger up*, where we should be more certain if it
began 'with the small'; a third Miltonism is *What time*, as if aspiring to
the Latin ablative phrase *quo tempore*. Although *a moment's space* allows
the inanimate *moment* to possess, in a way we think archaic, the idiom
has a limited currency still, as in 'an hour's time'. The Classical bits
here, and the mixed -*th*/-*s*, would be calmer amid a less conspicuous
vocabulary; but in a text not 190 years old we have a right to expect

Maid = 'maidservant', *eve* = 'night or day before', *grove* = 'two parallel lines of trees', *Full* = 'brimming'; *oft* and *fain* have gone, *deem* is ponderous or witty, *bid* (with its difficult verb forms) is unpopular, and *Mars* (in the active vocabulary of some) is limited for *me* to old ladies' saying things like 'How unpleasantness mars the afternoon', and the vignette in Hood's poems showing a horseman crashing through a five-bar with the caption 'A trip to Mar-gate'. We must fret a little further: *most* in the first line should show a superlative, another version of 'gentlest', but this occurrence is like the assertion of people that they are 'most grateful' for something. Amid all this, the sudden technical language of the child-psychologist – 'capable of no articulate sound' – adds its spot of anti-climax.

Admirers of JANE AUSTEN (1775–1817) make claims for her of perfection within a limited field; it may seem unfair to seek her in a graver, and even puzzled, mood which inhibited her completion of *The Watsons*, started in 1803 or 1804 but eventually abandoned before the period of her greatest novels. Its style is less assured, and correspondingly more artificial, than Jane Austen's at her best, but even here the elder Miss Watson, an imperfect character whose younger sister is back home after fourteen years in another household, is observed through pale green spectacles and gives herself away to us from our first acquaintance. Is she ever herself? – her odd idiom dominates the reunion as she sees her sister to the ball:

> 'Only observe whether she dances with Captain Hunter more than once – I have my fears in that quarter. Not that her father or mother like officers; but if she does, you know, it is all over with poor Sam. And I have promised to write him word who she dances with.'
> 'Is Sam attached to Miss Edwards?'
> 'Did not you know *that*?'
> 'How should I know it? How should I know in Shropshire what is passing of that nature in Surrey? It is not likely that circumstances of such delicacy should have made any part of the scanty communication which passed betwen you and me for the last fourteen years.'
> 'I wonder I never mentioned it when I wrote. Since you have been at home, I have been so busy with my poor father, and our

great wash, that I have had no leisure to tell you anything. . . . He has been very much in love with her these two years, and it is a great disappointment to him that he cannot always get away to our balls; but Mr. Curtis won't often spare him, and just now it is a sickly time at Guildford.'

I am perhaps being unfair not only to Jane Austen but to the reader, in presenting so raw and tentative a version of an author's omniscience, but even Miss Watson's bad grammar plays its part in her sulky attitude. She must stay at home to tend her sick old father ('my' father – as if her sister had no part in him), so she has 'some merit' (not a cordial phrase) in driving young Emma in the 'old chair' to the ball – the family cannot afford a 'close carriage'. Before the portion which I have quoted, she comes out with phrases which will sound more than 180 years old: Emma 'will hardly want partners' with so many officers around, which does *not* mean that she would obviously go for other ranks or civilians; their rich friend and frequent hostess 'has a very good taste', but with no cannibalistic reference; back *chez* Edwards, Emma will be 'sure of some comfortable soup', with no more idea of relaxing in it than in the 'comfortable words' of the Book of Common Prayer; Emma (some would now say, I fear, 'hopefully') should be 'in good looks', and perhaps even thought one of the prettiest there – 'there is a great deal in novelty' (*cat!*); Miss Watson would advise Emma 'by all means' not to encourage one Tom Musgrave, where 'by no means to' might sound a little easier; he had tried to flirt with Miss Watson when he 'came into this country' first (though not from abroad), and 'very great attention did he pay' her – an order which *does* at least give this attention prominence; the poor girl has 'not been very well used among' men, a phrase that has a gruff carnality surprising from her prim lips. These phrases are crammed into one page, but a strange pedestrianism comes over her speech, and the tartness and calculation suddenly leave her voice, as she reminisces (or romances) about lost loves, and nothing on which I would comment obtrudes for four pages, save (as they both put it) the awfulness of being 'teacher at a school', where we would prefer 'a teacher'.

Then as they approach the great house where Emma will be entertained before the ball, the plotting voice starts up again in the passage I quoted. *Only* might well be replaced by 'Just' (a French word, but no more elegant on account of that), and *in that quarter* has a practical mannish ring, perhaps because a mariner might thus refer to a threatening wind. Now the bad grammar starts: *father or mother* is singular, and requires the singular verb *likes*. The *does* is slightly ambiguous; it means, of course, *dances*, but could formally mean *likes*. We are nowadays told (I have never agreed) that you mustn't end a sentence with a preposition, but this *with* breaks the rule; far worse is the grammar of *who* for 'whom' – a correct dative form which has acquired bloated status now, as in 'Janet was there' – 'Janet whom?'. Kept as the direct or indirect object ('Whom did you see?' or 'To whom did you give it?') it is efficient. Suddenly stiff and formal, the elder sister says 'Did not you know that?', whereas there is plenty of proof of the vigour and politeness of 'Didn't'. This gets a slightly pompous reply, with *passing* for 'happening' or 'going on'; yet *made any part* is rather casual, and we prefer 'formed' or (with our liking for new verbs eked out with adverbs) 'made up'. Nor is Emma's sequence of tenses quite ours; we would let her speak of the 'communication which has passed' during the fourteen years which have only just ended, and which leave their effect on the present. Social changes have now obviated the steamy phrase *our great wash*, and the reason that Sam can't leave his medical duties at Guildford is that it is a *sickly time*, a much more sinister phrase (for some epidemic sweeping the place) than the present drab word 'sickly' suggests.

12 The Nineteenth Century: Various Affectations

GEORGE DARLEY (1795–1846) was a poet and mathematician; he even wrote on Italian art. Why he chose the style exemplified in the following extract from *Nepenthe* (1839), lines 234ff. and 465ff., is hard to say, and the idiom is not quite consistent; but revivals (even of Jacobean style) were in the air, and one of Darley's lyrics fooled Palgrave, the compiler of *The Golden Treasury*, who stuck it in the seventeenth century between poems by Milton and Carew.

> Light-trooping o'er the distant lea
> A band I saw, where Revelry
> Seem'd on her bacchant foot to be;
> And heard the dry tambour afar
> Before her Corybantian car
> Booming the rout to winy war . . .
> Uproar sweet! as when he crost,
> Omnipotent Bacchus, with his host,
> To farthest Ind; and for his van
> Satyrs and other sons of Pan,
> With swoln eye-burying cheeks of tan,
> Who troll'd him round, which way he ran
> His spotted yoke thro' Hindustan,
> And with most victorious scorn
> The mild foes of wine to warn,
> Blew his dithyrambic horn!
> That each river to his source
> Trembled and sank beneath his course,
> Where, 'tis said of many, they
> Mourn undiscover'd till this day . . .

This is hardly serious enough to warrant word-by-word analysis. Darley tries to authenticate the grammar by careful spelling: *Seem'd* (without the apostrophe, and with an *-e*, it would have two syllables; though by 1839 it would certainly *not*); *crost* (again, the pretence that *crossed* would have an extra syllable); *swoln* (but this really should be a disyllable – only Darley doesn't want it that way); *troll'd* and *undiscover'd* (as before). *Light-trooping* sounds traditional, but *eye-burying* is too shrewd and condensed to belong in the same tradition; *thro'* achieves nothing – it has a single syllable however you spell it, unless you go back to Shakespeare's 'Thorough bush, thorough brier, . . . Thorough flood, thorough fire' in *A Midsummer Night's Dream*; as for *o'er* and *lea* in the first line, they were neighbours in the second line of Gray's *Elegy*, and belong with all the other antique furniture of this synthetic style – the (now distracting) *car* and *van*, *rout* (not just a headlong retreat), *Ind* for 'India', *which way* more Latinate than our 'whichever way', *yoke* for a pair of yoked beasts, *That* for the current 'so that', the rivers seen as masculine with *his*, *'tis* (still comfortable in the South-West, but uneasy with words like *dithyrambic*), and *said of many* long displaced by 'said by many'. Little as I like this kind of thing, I admit that poor Darley (his life was as upset as his language) handles it very cleverly; he couldn't have guessed that a *band* would soon be instrumentalists only.

It would be easy, by selection from writings such as *Sartor Resartus*, to present a picture of THOMAS CARLYLE (1795–1881) as a perverse writer, but this oddity of style, warmed by the huge historical background and by compassion for so many sufferers, conveys his *French Revolution* in some of the most powerful, deliberate, word-by-word created prose in the language. Do not make it your model; only Carlyle's many idiosyncrasies can master it, and you will never need to tackle so foul an epic again (or so we may hope). But for the great moments it is superb:

> King Louis slept sound, till five in the morning, when Cléry, as he had been ordered, awoke him. Cléry dressed his hair: while this went forward, Louis took a ring from his watch, and kept trying it on his finger; it was his wedding-ring, which he is now to return to the Queen as a mute farewell. At half-past six, he took the Sacrament; and continued in devotion, and conference with Abbé Edgeworth. He will not see his Family; it were too hard to bear.

There are no fireworks here: the sentences and clauses are short; the vocabulary is familiar and simple, though four trisyllables come together at the time of the King's devotions, with a strange 'and conference' where 'and in conference' is expected. But everything is pared down: even *slept sound* is more demotic than 'soundly' would have made it, and *till* than *until*. The tenses zigzag; up to *wedding-ring*, it is all past tense, with one pluperfect as the correct backing, but now Louis *is* to return the ring; then he *took* the Sacrament, and again in the past *continued* at prayer. But he *will not*, reverting to the immediate present, because it *were* unbearable, the past subjunctive used as a conditional 'would be'. Informal phrases like *while this went forward* and *kept trying it on* maintain the awful ordinariness of this apparent death of a dynasty. But then a paragraph of broken prose begins, of various effects, matching the horrors grown real:

> At eight, the Municipals enter: the King gives them his Will, and messages and effects; which they, at first, brutally refuse to take charge of: he gives them a roll of gold pieces, a hundred and twenty-five louis; these are to be returned to Malesherbes, who had lent them. At nine, Santerre says the hour is come. The King begs yet to retire for three minutes. At the end of three minutes, Santerre again says the hour is come. 'Stamping on the ground with his right-foot, Louis answers: "*Partons*, let us go".' – How the rolling of those drums comes in, through the Temple bastions and bulwarks, on the heart of a queenly wife; soon to be a widow! He is gone, then, and has not seen us? A Queen weeps bitterly; a King's Sister and Children. Over all these Four does Death also hover: all shall perish miserably save one; she, as Duchesse d'Angoulême, will live, – not happily.

For no good reason, the first adjective clause (starting *which they*) is attached not by the usual comma but by a semi-colon; nor are the colons used as we are accustomed. The brutal Santerre twice conjugates the verb of motion, *come*, with the archaic *is* instead of *has*; and *yet* (for 'still') has an old-fashioned air also. I do not understand the hyphen in *right-foot*. As the door opens for them to step out, Carlyle cleverly diverts the sound of the drums immediately to Marie-Antoinette, and it is a verbal noun, *rolling*, which conveys it so well. We have been in the present tense throughout the paragraph, and the Queen is thinking in it, too: *He is gone, then?* The phrase *a King's Sister and Children* has an unexpressed *weep* for its verb; that Death should *hover* over them, that all but one must *perish miserably*, is not too pathetically expressed when we reflect that the Queen was judicially butchered, the saintly Madame Elizabeth similarly the year after, and the little Louis XVII we are not quite sure how.

The linguistics of concocted conversations are often well visualised; a good novelist will hear his puppets as clearly as he hears his acquaintances (who may well be the model for them). But it is surprising how often conversations supposedly authentic are reported in a non-language as unconvincing as the way that D. H. Lawrence's characters talk at one another. I think GEORGE BORROW (1803–1881) is important in this connexion: he was obviously a tireless talker, and mistook this for being a great conversationalist; every word had to be recalled and printed, the result being incredibly stylised – when the gist could have been quite lively; in *Wild Wales* (1862), a book which most Welshmen like myself regard as pretty hateful (though acknowledging his skill and energy in learning Welsh), he gives himself the extra task of reproducing Welsh conversations in a kind of funny English (which Welsh is *not*), made worse by his bossy and prying tone and his obvious pleasure in slapping down any native who argues. But the entertainment value of these encounters is, for various wrong reasons, huge. I quote from the delightful Collins illustrated edition by Cecil Price (1964): on p. 123 Borrow inflicts himself on two cottagers. It is a fine Sunday morning.

> After I had been gazing a little time a man making his appearance at the door of the cottage just beyond the bridge I passed on [probably Borrow *talked* without commas, too], and drawing nigh to him, after a slight salutation, asked him in English the name of the bridge [*nigh* is pretentious, the salutation could have been before the drawing or after it, and it is clear that Borrow didn't bestow proper salutations on the unquizzed peasantry].
> 'The name of the bridge, sir', said the man, in very good English, 'is Pont y Pandy'.
> 'Does not that mean the bridge of the fulling mill?'
> 'I believe it does, sir', said the man.
> 'Is there a fulling mill near?'
> 'No, sir, there was one some time ago, but it is now a sawing mill'.

[However carefully they were sparring with one another, this strikes me as far too stilted to be real; they would surely have said 'Doesn't' and 'it's'.]

Here a woman, coming out, looked at me steadfastly.

'Is that gentlewoman your wife?'

'She is no gentlewoman, sir, but she is my wife'.

'Of what religion are you?'

'We are Calvinistic-Methodists, sir'.

'Have you been to chapel?'

'We are just returned, sir' . . .

[This shows the verb of motion still conjugated with *be* instead of *have*; and on Temple Meads Station, Bristol, the announcers still say 'The train now arrived at platform 3 is the 8.20 for . . . .', which has the effect of giving the participle its purely adjectival force].

'Have you been to chapel, sir?'

'I do not go to chapel; I belong to the Church'.

'Have you been to church, sir?'

'I have not – I said my prayers at home, and then walked out'.

'It is not right to walk out on the Sabbath day, except to go to church or chapel'.

'Who told you so?'

'The law of God, which says you shall keep holy the Sabbath day'.

'I am not keeping it unholy'.

'You are walking about, and in Wales when we see a person walking idly about, on the Sabbath day, we are in the habit of saying "Sabbath breaker, where are you going?" '

'The Son of Man walked through the fields on the Sabbath day, why should I not walk along the roads?'

[This comma is not adequate as punctuation].

'He who called Himself the Son of Man was God, and could do what He pleased, but you are not God'.

'But He came in the shape of a man to set an example. Had there been anything wrong in walking about on the Sabbath day, He would not have done it'.

Here the wife exclaimed, 'How worldly-wise these English are!'

'You do not like the English', said I.

'We do not dislike them', said the woman; 'at the present they do us no harm, whatever they did of old'.

'But you still consider them,' said I, 'The seed of Y Sarfes cadwynog, the coiling serpent'.

'I should be loth to call any people the seed of the serpent', said the woman.

'But one of your great bards did', said I.

'He must have belonged to the Church, and not to the chapel then', said the woman. 'No person who went to chapel would have used such bad words'.

This is all too neat, a witty invention rather than genuine record; yet Borrow's ponderousness may well have imposed order on the speech of those whom he challenged. For 'the little freckled maid' at Bala (p. 357) his 'A'n't' for *are not* was presumably good enough, and she replies with a ''Cause' for *because*, and the vulgar form 'convarting'. Yet his conversations rarely take the forms we would expect, partly because he is not very free with 'please' or 'thank you', and because his voracious questions plod off at so many tangents. Even a tender moment may be framed to accommodate a religious epigram; the blind Catherine Hughes (p. 127), 'Fifteen after three twenties' years old, on her stool at the cottage door, has not been left alone by her family on their going to chapel: 'They left me with my God'.

13 Tennyson

To write merely of the voices of ALFRED, LORD TENNYSON (1804–1892), their music and their demonstration of 'the finest ear of any English poet' (T. S. Eliot, 1936), would be irrelevant to this book; but if it can be shown that this varied music tapped the many linguistic resources of our language, then it is straight to our point. *In Memoriam* (1849), to lovers of theological and philosophical niceties, may appear to have a confused thesis, and this is all the more marked through being conveyed in such a cleared air; for here is the first sustained, deliberate use of a stark (which in Old English meant 'strong' or 'stiff') style, cold and dead in sound for the most part, but often fevered and intense. It is economical in diction, and markedly Old English; whole stanzas, and almost whole cantos, will be without Romance words, and the movement is thus staccato and mono-syllabic, as in the line that T. S. Eliot admired, 'On the bald street breaks the blank day'. With this goes an almost affected simplicity of sentence-structure, without grammatical fireworks or abuses of word-order; not that revolutionary quirks of language are to be expected in 1849, but the diction here has what *must* be a studied, self-conscious return to something less obviously clever than the unending influence of Milton or the infection of the early Romantics. It is work to a formula.

IX

Fair ship, that from the Italian shore
  Sailest the placid ocean-plains
  With my lost Arthur's loved remains,
Spread thy full wings, and waft him o'er.

(This is a tribute to the old idiom; nothing could be more Latinate than those three successive words *placid ocean-plains*; the antiquated

94

fair for 'beautiful', the 2nd person singular verb in *-est*, *waft*, and *o'er*, all belong in the tradition, though Tennyson can no longer pretend that *loved* needs to be spelt *lov'd*).

> So draw him home to those that mourn
>> In vain; a favourable speed
>> Ruffle thy mirror'd mast, and lead
> Thro' prosperous floods his holy urn.

(This is similar, but more wilful. After a line like a metronome, there is a run-on of two single syllables, and then the big words can begin, along with an observer's view of the sailing-ship, her mast zigzagging across the rippling, reflecting sea; and here is a figure of speech, the transferred epithet whereby the prosperous journey has its characteristic turned to the ocean instead. But why *mirror'd*? – Tennyson is suddenly pretending that it would otherwise risk being pronounced *mirrorèd*; *Thro'* achieves nothing – no one was now pronouncing *through* as *'throokh'*; *floods* were by now water in the wrong place, not just leagues of water; the subjunctives *Ruffle* and *lead* were dying from common use; and cremation had not yet been introduced, so that the *urn* is a mere antique adornment. It is all as much as to say 'This is poetry, and we must get it over before we set in it our inmost feelings'; the archaisms still include a recourse to grammar).

> All night no ruder air perplex
>> Thy sliding keel, till Phosphor, bright
>> As our pure love, thro' early light
> Shall glimmer on the dewy decks.

(Still obdurate, the poet produces another subjunctive, *perplex*; the ship is still 2nd person singular with *thy*; the morning 'star' has to be called Phosphor – though everyone by then knew that it was Venus; and *thro'* is repeated. The *dewy decks* offer hope of something fresher and more natural).

> Sphere all your lights around, above;
>> Sleep, gentle heavens, before the prow;
>> Sleep, gentle winds, as he sleeps now,
> My friend, the brother of my love;

(An appearance of calm is induced by the tranquil words *Sphere* and *Sleep*, and by the frank repetition of *gentle*; and the last twelve words are native, though expressing the evasive description of the dead Hallam as if he were Tennyson's fiancée's brother, not the fiancé of Tennyson's sister).

> My Arthur, whom I shall not see
>   Till all my widow'd race be run;
>   Dear as the mother to the son,
> More than my brothers are to me.

(An entirely Old English vocabulary, the last two lines passionately bleak and simple, the only little concessions to 'poesy' being the added apostrophe in *widow'd* and the subjunctive *be*. The next canto works quite differently).

X

> I hear the noise about thy keel;
>   I hear the bell struck in the night:
>   I see the cabin-window bright,
> I see the sailor at the wheel.

(The sickness and barrenness is here succeeded by a warm impressionism; the diction is almost all native, the parallelism as Hebraic as a Psalm; the ship is still being addressed, which is growing tiresome, and still needs *thy* as if in some ritual, but the four little vignettes have the spindrift in their nostrils and help to relieve the clamminess of the previous canto).

> Thou bring'st the sailor to his wife,
>   And travell'd men from foreign lands;
>   And letters unto trembling hands;
> And, thy dark freight, a vanish'd life.

(The parallelism continues, but to a gloomy climax. The Latinate words have increased, but little enough in 'poetic' content, save that the shore is near now, and we must consider the more sophisticated elements of the voyage – the sailor's other existence, the globe-trotters, the mail. From all these Tennyson is cut off; Hallam's body is the only reality. He is still insisting on that *'d*, and has to use the ugly elided *bring'st* to get his syllables right).

> So bring him: we have idle dreams:
>   This look of quiet flatters thus
>   Our home-bred fancies: O to us,
> The fools of habit, sweeter seems

> To rest beneath the clover sod,
>   That takes the sunshine and the rains,
>   Or where the kneeling hamlet drains
> The chalice of the grapes of God;

(These two stanzas introduce a new element – argument and rationalisation – quite frequent and often unwelcome in the poem. Yet the first six lines prove to be the prelude to the 'fine phrase' – which I also feel *is* a really fine phrase in its own right – where Clevedon is seen as focused in worship at the old St Andrew's church, and sharing the chalice and its wine; the intense beauty of these two lines is dependent largely on the vowel harmony of their seven stressed words: *where, kneeling, hamlet, drains, chalice, (of), grapes, God* – the high vowels $\hat{e}$, *ee*, *æ*, *é*, *æ*, *é*, and then the stunning surprise of the low back vowel *o*).

> Than if with thee the roaring wells
>   Should gulf him fathom-deep in brine;
>   And hands so often clasp'd in mine
> Should toss with tangle and with shells.

(Tennyson shows no concern for the crew and passengers; the ship may sink, and he is worried lest Hallam should not be buried in Clevedon churchyard; but the wording is handsome – this time with the consonant harmony of the last line: *t . . . ss . . . t . . . l . . . sh . . . lz*).

The fumbling argument (as many judge it) of the whole poem, the destructive use of conversation, the hapless discussion on what kind of nieces and nephews Hallam might have begotten for Tennyson, is often matched in the wording. Yet canto LVI, which starts with fossils and the weird line *'So careful of the type?' but no*, contains the famous *Nature, red in tooth and claw* and sees dead men *seal'd within the iron hills*. The insistent recurring voice of loss and unfulfilment is close always to the bleak native diction of A. E. Housman, and *For all is dark where thou art not* (VIII) is only just too smooth for *A Shropshire Lad*, which might use it without the *For*. A sound – but a grammatical inflexion too – which Tennyson exploits is the *-ing* (mostly in its use as verbal noun). The first stanza of canto CXXX exemplifies this well, though the emphasis is here on present participles:

> Thy voice is on the rolling air;
>   I hear thee where the waters run;
>   Thou standest in the rising sun,
> And in the setting Thou art fair.

The first line has all its operative words from French, the other three have none at all. The last two lines form that very Classical and mediaeval figure, the chiasmus: verb, adverb phrase, adverb phrase, verb. The second line is a deliberate verb concept (the waters are active) instead of a more obvious noun concept 'by the waters'. Above all, there are two *-ing* participles, *rolling* and *rising*, and a lovely ambiguous participle or verbal noun in the last line.

The same inflexion informs a whole line of *The Princess*, that blank-verse story relieved by beautiful lyrics, one of which runs:

> As thro' the land at eve we went,
>   And pluck'd the ripen'd ears,
> We fell out, my wife and I,
> O we fell out, I know not why,
>   And kiss'd again with tears.
> And blessings on the falling out
>   That all the more endears,
> When we fall out with those we love,
>   And kiss again with tears! . . .

This pair of verbal nouns, *blessings* and *falling*, has an inexplicable charm; the rest is pretty but artificial – *thro'*, *eve*, the unnecessary apostrophe in *pluck'd*, *ripen'd*, *kiss'd*, even the revival of *know not*. Within the compass of 47 lines in *The Princess* occur the notoriously clever 'small / Sweet Idyl', *Come down, O maid, from yonder mountain height*, all onomatopoeia, and the sublime unrhymed lyric

Now sleeps the crimson petal, now the white;
Nor waves the cypress in the palace walk;
Nor winks the gold fin in the porphyry font:
The fire-fly wakens; waken thou with me.

Now droops the milkwhite peacock like a ghost,
And like a ghost she glimmers on to me.

Now lies the earth all Danaë to the stars,
And all thy heart lies open unto me.

Now slides the silent meteor on, and leaves
A shining furrow, as thy thoughts in me.

Now folds the lily all her sweetness up,
And slips into the bosom of the lake:
So fold thyself, my dearest, thou, and slip
Into my bosom and be lost in me.

Tennyson emphasises in the first of these two poems 'Sweeter thy voice, but every sound is sweet', so it is indeed all pretty noises like

Myriads of rivulets hurrying thro' the lawn,
The moan of doves in immemorial elms,
And murmuring of innumerable bees.

This is finely 'crafted', as people say now, but how much more moving is the little rhymeless picture of evening! It conveys a calm and privileged life, in which nothing would ever go wrong, no servant ever be lacking to sweep the sanded walks, a life intercepted and immortalised for our comfort, not for our envy, in this jewel of a poem. Its methods are various.

There is economy in *Nor waves*, which we have lost in favour of 'does not wave'; metonymy (part for whole) in *Nor winks the gold fin*; the onomatopoeia of silence in the 3 *s*s, the 2 *p*s, the 2 *l*s, of *Now sleeps the crimson petal*; a remembered flicker to show the utter calm that has now set in, with *porphyry*; the sudden thrill of allusion in an immensely compressed style, *Now lies the earth all Danaë to the stars*, where Danaë, visited in her tower by her lover as a shower of gold, is wrenched from a proper name into an adjective; the shock of mystery in the hushed line *Now slides the silent meteor on*, the gigantic meteor's silence being its sinister feature. But the grammar is strangely 'normal', save for the deeply personal *thou*.

14   Emily Dickinson

Three of the subtlest and most effective elements in the style of
EMILY DICKINSON (1830–1886, remaining all her life at
Amherst, Massachusetts) are linguistic – the assonance of imperfect
rhymes, the distinctive functions of English and Romance vocabulary, and the grammar. More emphasis, too, should be laid on her use
of hymn-measures; she did not use them in sincere imitation of
hymnody, her religious upbringing having inured her against their
often trivial lilt, but it was not just in parody, either – it was simply the
kind of metre to which her ear had grown accustomed. The
rhyme-and-stress scheme *abcb* 4343, and the only slightly less
familiar *abcb* 3343, are as common in hymnals as in her 1,775 poems,
and they impose on her verses a simplicity that veils depth and
complexity. Very often she 'pointed' her poems with her own strange
system of punctuation: James Reeves, in his excellent edition of 181
poems (London: Heinemann, 1959), omits this pointing, and indeed
it is hard to print it with consistency.

Short lines, then, and jerky rhythms, pared diction, slurred
rhymes, with one conspicuous feature of grammar – what are either
meant as subjunctives or dressed up (*down* really, with the loss of *-s*) as
subjunctives. Recall, of course, that you can tell a subjunctive only in
the 3rd person singular present; all other forms, save *be* throughout
the present and *were* in the past singular, are the same as the
indicative. In view of this, it is surprising that so many occur in her
poetry: does she take a subjunctive view of things? I feel that one of her
apparent subjunctives, at least, is just a rustic New England
indicative still familiar in rural England, in the poem that begins 'Too
few the morning be'; but most of them belong to her many hours of
uncertainty and speculation. Reeves realises that to her the truth is
'often provisional', and so her combined reticence and her feeling that

it is 'delightful to tell' the truth produce the subjunctive 'mood', where the grammarian's word aptly coincides with another.

Are her subjunctives, then, for tentative main statements whereas indicatives are for confident reports? A hard case to judge would be the trenchant stanzas which Reeves quotes:

> They say that time assuages.
>   Time never did assuage.
> An actual suffering strengthens
>   As sinews do, with age.
>
> Time is a test of trouble
>   But not a remedy.
> If such it prove, it prove too
>   There was no malady.

Three indicatives in *-s* (*assuages*, *strengthens*, *is*) are suddenly forgotten in an *if*-clause with the subjunctive *prove* (as had been customary), followed by a main statement with the subjunctive *prove*; and this last had not been customary, even though one find its excuse that it has been 'attracted' by the previous *prove*.

What a dying eye may be looking for is the setting for two subjunctives in the last lines of:

> I've seen a dying eye
>   Run round and round a room,
> In search of something, as it seemed,
>   Then cloudier become,
> And then obscure with fog,
>   And then, be soldered down,
> Without disclosing what it be
>   Were blessed to have seen.

Here, the pathetic caprice of a dying loved one, in trying to express, or allot, or arrange, some addled idea that once meant much, is sadly left to grammar's hesitant mood. In 'A Word dropped careless on a Page', in T. H. Johnson, *The Complete Poems of Emily Dickinson* (London: Faber, 1975), No. 1261, 'When . . . The Wrinkled Maker Lie' shows a subjunctive after *when* for something which is bound to happen; this is strange, but we could go back to Middle English and claim that this is the frequent use of *when* for 'whenever' + the subjunctive. But the search for explanations is sometimes baffled, as when Emily says straightforwardly

> I never saw a moor,
>   I never saw the sea,
> Yet know I how the heather looks
>   And what a billow be.

There is one tiny possibility: whereas a billow *is*, just as much as the heather *looks*, the fact that it is only a passing, single billow confers the mood on it. And what is meant when the soul (and here we must haplessly keep the pointing and perhaps the capitals)

> Unmoved . . . notes the Chariots – pausing –
>   At her low Gate –
> Unmoved – an Emperor be kneeling
>   Upon her Mat –?

This third line needs only inversion ('be an Emperor kneeling') to make it conditional; certainly, she 'notes the Chariots pausing' is not a construction parallel to '(she notes) an Emperor *be* kneeling'. One of her most famous poems – even the old *Oxford Dictionary of Quotations* (1941–) included its last two lines as her only contribution – has a plain example of *If* preceding a subjunctive:

> My life closed twice before its close.
>   It yet remains to see
> If immortality unveil
>   A third event to me,
>
> So huge, so hopeless to conceive
>   As these that twice befell.
> Parting is all we know of heaven,
>   And all we need of hell.

Normal in its *if*-clause, correct in its *b*-rhymes, this poem is made more satisfying by its neat (yet inexorable) rhythm and its three alliterations in the second stanza, on *h* and finally on the sounds *n*, *h*, *n*, *h*. It concerns – so it is usually believed – the departure and, later, the distant death of someone whom she loved intensely; as perhaps the

most 'important' poem she ever wrote, it has taken on a polished
perfection unusual in her work. In 'I heard a fly buzz', her statement
that she

> Signed away
> What portion of me be
> Assignable,

the use of the subjunctive is traditional, but what exactly is the
function of the repeated forms of it in

> The Robin is the one
> That interrupt the morn –

'The robin is just the one who *would* interrupt'? It recurs twice in the
same little poem – 'That overflow', 'That . . . submit', but a final main
clause, which is plural, has *are*. In some of the more perverse poems,
like 'The Mushroon is the elf of plants', there is a seemingly pointless
mixture of 'It stop upon a spot' and 'Doth', the improvised and the
archaic.

This subjunctive (or whatever it sometimes is) is her principal
linguistic oddity. She admittedly had some unorthodox grammar
besides; words like *gallanter*, *durabler*, ellipses like

> Reckon the morning's flagons up
> And say how many dew,

and in 'Still own thee' the compounds *reportless* and *recallless* (three *l*s
and all) within five lines. All the easier, then, were the bizarre
expressions:

> A quartz contentment, like a stone –
> This is the hour of lead;

and painfully easy were the lines to shock, about God's 'amputated'
hand or, an extreme example,

> I like a look of agony
> Because I know it's true;
> or   Water is taught by thirst;
> or   Finer is a going than a remaining face;

this last resembles something we have seen in other writers, the haunting echo of two verbal nouns or present participles in -*ing*, or even (in Emily's poetry) one or more of each:

> Summer has two beginnings,
>   Beginning once in June,
> Beginning in October,
>   Affectingly again

– where I feel that the -*ing* of *Affectingly* is overstaying its welcome. But the verbal noun is (for some elusive reason) more powerful than another mere noun would be in

> First chill, then stupor, then the letting go,

and in that house the morning after death:

> The sweeping up the heart
>   And putting love away
> We shall not want to use again
>   Until Eternity

It is astonishing that as we debate her dependence on linguistic tricks or on a linguistic policy, she has some news for us in a cheerful long poem of 1862 called 'Going to him! Happy letter!' It must:

> Tell him the page I didn't write –
> Tell him – I only said the syntax –
> And left the verb and the pronoun out –

a confident method, but not a helpful one.

One vital aspect of her art, as it shades into the linguistic framework, is the use of half-rhymes which, in a manner so daring for her day, take the place very often of pure rhymes. Reeves wisely left open the question whether they reacted against the jingle of hymns or joined the subjunctives in their reticence and doubt. I should favour the latter theory, and take some of them even into the realms of despair; well, perhaps this is too strong an emotion to apply to her, but some of her quatrains are very like Hamlet's

For thou dost know, O Damon dear,
   This realm dismembered was
Of Jove himself; and now reigns here
   A very, very . . . paiocke.

Horatio saves the editors from countless emendations by saying sadly
'You might have rimed'.

The desultory form of these off-rhymes comes out in all seven
stanzas of Emily's great poem on the death of a woman; even the
b-rhyme of the fourth is falsified in its stress and quantity.

The last night that she lived,
   It was a common night
Except the dying – this to us
   Made nature different.

We noticed smallest things,
   Things overlooked before,
By this great light upon our minds
   Italicised, as 'twere.

As we went out and in
   Between her final room
And rooms where those to be alive
   Tomorrow were, a blame

That others could exist
   While she must finish quite,
A jealousy for her arose
   So nearly infinite.

We waited while she passed;
   It was a narrow time.
Too jostled were our souls to speak.
   At length the notice came.

She mentioned, and forgot;
   Then lightly as a reed
Bent to the water, struggled scarce,
   Consented, and was dead.

And we, we placed the hair
   And drew the head erect;
And then an awful leisure was,
   Belief to regulate.

First of all, whereas the rhymes don't obey the usual discipline, the stress-scheme is rigid in each stanza: 3 3 4 3, like so many hymns (e.g. George Herbert's 'Teach me, my God and King'). Alliteration is hardly brought into play. The beginning is as simple and repetitive as a ballad ('The last night . . . It was a common night'), with a delicate understatement: 'usual kind of night except for a death' – but *death* is not used, and instead the more poignant verbal noun *dying* adds its force. She is employing business-like words without any coyness: rather stuffy Romance words like *different*, *noticed*, *italicised* – it simply isn't an occasion for funerary small-talk. And, as if apologetic about her far-fetched application of *italicised*, she capsizes quite humanly with *as 'twere* (which we would use facetiously now). The guilt about staying alive takes up, reasonably, two stanzas, and the dying woman is bluntly seen as 'finishing' and soon as 'passing'. The notice, which is not a normal notice stuck up, is the signal for a stanza of wonderful compassion but of realism, too, where the woman 'mentioned' something without a direct object to her verb, as if the core of the action were right out of it, then gave way to the waterfloods about her (such as Emily often used as a symbol of eternity) and 'consented' – again, emptily, to nothing deducible from grammar. And then they did the right things, and blamelessly took some 'leisure'.

15 Late Victorian Experimentation

I must admit my dislike of THOMAS HARDY (1840–1928) as novelist; I could dislike any writer who ended so cruel a book (you may call it compassionate if you wish) as *Tess* with a snidely intruded character called The President of the Immortals. But his lyrics, which happily took over when *Jude* shrivelled up the last of his fictional impulse in 1896, not only convince me but may contain something to our more pedantic purpose; his interest in true Dorset speech, and peasant directness or evasiveness, must often be in tension with the formal stanzaic verse which he practised. I have found the collection *Human Shows: Far Phantasies* (London: Macmillan, 1925) of some interest here, though Hardy does not habitually take a theme and 'make it strange' for poetry. But 'Last Week in October' (p. 19) has just two stanzas, the first light and simple, with a dependence on the one idea of the increasing nakedness of the trees, the other archaic and contrived, as if by a different writer:

> The trees are undressing, and fling in many places –
>   On the gray road, the roof, the window-sill
> Their radiant robes and ribbons and yellow laces;
>   A leaf each second so is flung at will,
> Here, there, another and another, still and still.
>
> A spider's web has caught one while downcoming,
>   That stays there dangling when the rest pass on;
> Like a suspended criminal hangs he, mumming,
>   In golden garb, while one yet green, high yon,
> Trembles, as fearing such a fate for himself anon.

No special effect is switched on in the first stanza save the thrice-alliterating *r*- in line 3. But the second stanza won't do at all; the image of the hanged criminal (why can't he *say* 'hanged'? — nowadays, of course, we instinctively think of the 'suspended sentence') awakes no response; billions of leaves are *not* pitiful or 'like' hanged men. And talking of 'dangling', that is just what the folksy word 'downcoming' is doing; it dangles between reference to the web and to a leaf — after all, spiders' webs *do* float around; 'mumming' — for 'whispering, keeping silence, playing dumbshow' — will just about do, since the leaf is given golden fancy dress; 'Yon' is folksy again, and the strained image of the nervous leaf is of a piece with the mistaken and archaic 'anon' — which really meant 'at once', and not 'eventually' as we now facetiously use it.

Quaint notions and quaint words, with rich trochaic rhymes in every line, form the whimsical yet wry 'Green Slates':

> It happened once, before the duller
>   Loomings of life defined them,
> I searched for slates of greenish colour
>   A quarry where men mined them.
>
> And saw, the while [*quo tempore*!] I peered around
>   there,
>   In the quarry standing [this 'dangles' too]
> A form against the slate background there
>   Of fairness eye-commanding. [a just, mediocre,
>   blonde?]
>
> And now, though fifty years have flown me [*from* me],
>   With all their dreams and duties,
> And strange-pipped dice my hand has thrown me,
>   And dust are all her beauties,
>
> Green slates — seen high on roofs, or lower
>   In waggon, truck, or lorry —
> Cry out: 'Our home was where you saw her
>   Standing in the quarry!'

The ordinary — pips on dice, lorries — are the furniture of a life summed up in that intense and harrowing phrase 'dreams and duties'; Hardy batted on to 88, with all the more time for regret that

he had ever met, married and lost Emma Gifford. Here he hits on the
right idiom for saying as much.

When he calls a poem 'Night-Time in Mid-Fall', it is no surprise
when it starts with another compound, but the first two lines are
inexcusable:

>   It is a storm-strid night, winds footing swift
>   Through the blind profound.

The use of 'swift' for the adverb 'swiftly' is a mere poeticism; the
closing phrase means 'blind profundity' or 'profound blindness';
'storm-strid' must mean 'marched through by storms'. The *Shorter
Oxford English Dictionary* (1933 onwards), which always keeps room
for the best, does not include *strid* as the past participle of *to stride*, only
stridden; Longman's *Contemporary dictionary* (1978) gives *stridden* in the
entry, but *stridden* or *strid* in a table of irregular verbs at the end; and
then in 1962 the *Oxford Illustrated Dictionary* suddenly gives *strode* as the
only form (sharing it with the past tense). What are we to make of
these anomalies? – they are signs, alas, that all rarely used irregular
verbs are slithering into the regular conjugation, which is a polite way
of saying that they are becoming blurred. The form which will
reconcile *stridden*, *strid*, *strode* is the 'regular' *strided*, and even Boswell
was saying *he strided* for the past tense two hundred years ago.

When Hardy is in this mood of linguistic pretence, and also hunting
for analogies, the results can be very silly. In 'A Light Snow-Fall after
Frost', he sees a man coming by with a red beard and a green coat;
fatuous in wording as in ideas, the lines grind out:

>   Hence seems it that his mien
>   Wears something of the dye
>   Of the berried holm-trees that he passes nigh;

'hence', the reversed 'it seems', 'mien', 'nigh' for 'near', and even the
unfamiliar 'holm' for 'holm-oak', make this into unenjoyable verse.
By Hardy's time we meet few violations of grammar in formal writing,
but when, years after Emma's death, he passes the greenhouse at St
Juliot where they forgot the stove one bitter night, and in the morning
she looked scared and tragic, he calls it (in 'The Frozen Greenhouse')
the place *Of her once dismay*, which I like little apart from its economy;
but the poem is tragic, and does not ask for pithy phrases. Similarly,

the human dilemma is ill conveyed in the poem that takes its title from the first two lines,

> Freed the fret of thinking,
>   Light of lot were we;

'freed' for 'freed from' was once passable, 'light of lot' can be glossed mentally into 'having an easy time of it', the past subjunctive 'were' to mean 'would be' has a venerable but elderly record, and the inversion of pronoun and verb in 'were we' is allowable for the sake of the rhyme. But what chance has sincerity amid all this? – predictably, the poem wriggles on for its 21 lines as if through a pool of glue.

I was early disillusioned with GERARD MANLEY HOPKINS (1844–1889) as a 'daring linguistic and metrical innovator'. He was pitted against Tennyson, compared with the new minds of their ages (Donne or Eliot) when Swinburne and Keats and Ruskin and Pater were really the looming influences, made into an honorary twentieth-century poet, praised for his exploitation of inscape (the thisness of things) and its effect on his instress, and credited with discovering 'sprung' rhythm – a term for something he certainly did not invent, with new compound nouns ascribed to him which turn out to be simply two words (or even three) run together in a way that does not enrich their meaning. The elements that one might expect are missing in his diction; for someone who changed from the Church of England to Roman Catholicism at 22, and entered the Jesuits at 24, the lack of a Biblical or liturgical language is striking, and there is a curious lack of discipline in many of his 'compounds'.

The most successful of his purely linguistic devices is the accumulation of fine phrases; *The Wreck of the Deutschland* has many:

> And the sea flint-flake, black-backed in the
>   regular blow,
> Sitting Eastnortheast, in cursed quarter, the wind;
> Wiry and white-fiery and whirlwind-swivellèd snow
> Spins to the widow-making unchilding unfathering deeps.

Here again the *-ing* inflexion releases its special power; but the music is Swinburne's in his *Armada*, no model for a Jesuit. And sometimes the only merit of such a list is compression, at the cost of being misunderstood even with notes by Hopkins, Bridges, W. H. Gardner, and Jesuits who were experts on the Father or on the portion of Ignatius Loyola that lay behind the excerpt; see what Yvor Winters, a very cool witness, does to 'The Windhover' in *The Function of Criticism*. The fine, new phrases, too, can be replaced by strange concatenations of words such as 'two-fro tender trambeams truckle at the eye'; the compounds may be exciting, like the *dapple-dawn-drawn Falcon* in 'The Windhover', where the octet of the sonnet contains eleven words ending in that attractive *-ing*, but they may leave us with an impression of their futility, as with *mansex* in 'The Bugler's First Communion'. This sickly and perhaps secretive poem provides words that will shock, in a contrived metric that will not please:

> A bugler boy from barrack (it is over the hill
> There) – boy bugler, born, he tells me, of Irish
>   Mother to an English sire (he
> Shares their best gifts surely, fall how things will),
>
> This very very day came down to us after a boon he on
> My late being there begged of me, overflowing
>   Boon in my bestowing,
> Came, I say, this day to it – to a First Communion.
>
> Here he knelt then in regimental red.
> Forth Christ from cupboard fetched, how fain I of feet
>   To his youngster take his treat!
> Low-latched in leaf-light housel his too huge
>   godhead.

There is an inappropriate mixture of homely proverb – *fall* (subjunctive) *how things will*; colloquial prattle – *very very*; prepositions – seven in the second stanza; comic rhymes – *Irish* and *sire he Sh-* and (as if from a limerick) *boon he on* and *Communion*; jolly schoolboy words – *youngster* and *treat*; a sturdy but insensitive statement of the Real Presence – *Christ from cupboard*; and some archaisms to dilute the modernism – *fain* and *housel*. Hopkins says it cheers him to see

> . . . limber liquid youth, that to all I teach
>   Yields tender as a pushed peach;

and he rejoices to serve God by serving to

>Just such slips of soldiery Christ's royal ration.

Not surprisingly, a colleague of mine has described the poem, with some help from *Macbeth*, as 'supernatural solicitings'.

In the twentieth century, writers with the enormous vision of James Joyce in *Finnegans Wake* have erected whole stretches of syntaxless words, wrenched grammar, fused words, sentences unbegun and unended, and all to imaginative purpose. Most of Hopkins's violations of syntax look tame now, and to no purpose for the most part. The same vision could have been expressed conventionally instead of that aspect of Harry Ploughman,

>See his wind-lilylocks-laced;
>Churlsgrace, too, child of Amansstrength . . . .;

yet when this kind of trick is controlled, Hopkins can use it with a strength that can produce a popular and still deeply personal line, as when he sees how Felix Randal the blacksmith

>at the random grim forge, powerful amidst peers,
>Didst fettle for the great grey drayhorse his bright
>and battering sandal!

The sonnet that ends 'leaves me a lonely began' is a desperate cry, but no more sincere for fading into an impossible piece of syntax, for which an analogy with 'woebegone' is one of several unsatisfactory readings; as it stands, the indefinite article *a* + the adjective *lonely* cannot possibly precede the past tense *began*. In *The Loss of the Eurydice*, a spun-out, sentimental account of an 1878 foundering, with lines like

>lovely manly mould,
>Every inch a tar,
>Of the best we boast our sailors are,

with its ludicrous reminder of 'Well, you know what sailors are!', he saves the worst linguistic restlessness to the end. After apostrophizing the bereaved –

O well wept, mother have lost son;
  Wept, wife; wept, sweetheart would be one

(where the omitted *who* with the ?subjunctive *have*, *well* before the second *wept*, and *who* after *sweetheart*, do no damage) – he ends a prayer to Christ with 'O Hero savest'. This is pointless: 'O Hero that savest' would not impair the rhythm, and as it stands *savest* is merely an indicative, not an imperative.

A. E. HOUSMAN (1859–1936) is perhaps the easiest poet in this book to categorize linguistically. He was the greatest Classical scholar that the nation has produced, yet in his poems he was a not wholly realised Shropshire peasant, and even when his longest verse-sequence ended, his other poems, all short, had the same gloomy protagonist, grown educated, lurking inside them. And the English was appropriate: utterly simple, almost bare of Latin and Greek words (so that when one occurs, it glitters), and as far from the acrimonious Classical scholar and critic as its author could escape. The dichotomy is tragic in its origins, but if we can forget the professor and the pedant, who have no business in *A Shropshire Lad*, the English poetry is as clear as any ever written, sustained largely by mono-syllables. Here is the twelfth of its sixty-three parts:

When I watch the living meet,
  And the moving pageant file
Warm and breathing through the street
  Where I lodge a little while,

If the heats of hate and lust
  In the house of flesh are strong,
Let me mind the house of dust
  Where my sojourn shall be long.

In the nation that is not
  Nothing stands that stood before;
There revenges are forgot,
  And the hater hates no more;

Lovers lying two and two
  Ask not whom they sleep beside,
And the bridegroom all night through
  Never turns him to the bride.

Yet, without calling this 'deceptive simplicity', I know that *something* must be said to amplify the desperate reticence. Of the words, only one-tenth are from Latin (*via* French), and there is nothing scholarly about most of them; only *sojourn*, almost sarcastically used amid monosyllables, has any affectation about it, and *lodge* even has a hint of vulgarity, lodgings not being for the best people. The native word *mind* (for *remember*) is still good Scots ('D'ye mind?', they say, with no hint of an apology); *forgot* is a concession to an antiquated form of the participle; *Ask not* is an ideal – but lost – construction; and *him* for the reflexive is a final piece of mediaeval speech. What is quaint here, Housman could claim, is so because it is rustic, but the danger of parody for this kind of hill-billy expression was great, and he incurred it in such venomous imitations as

> What, still alive at twenty-two,
> A fine upstanding lad like you?

Yet have unbelief, despair, the impermanence of love, and the finality of death, ever been better stated than in those four little quatrains? The futility of war has never been summed up better than in this sensible, caddish war memorial poem of a mere forty syllables and a mere two exotic words (*-cause* and *sure*, which we would not notice as French and imported):

> Here dead lie we because we did not choose
> To live and shame the land from which we sprung.
> Life, to be sure, is nothing much to lose;
> But young men think it is, and we were young.

Grammatically, there is of course one aberration here – *sprung* for 'sprang'; or so we now say – but 'sprang' is properly the past singular, and the past plural was 'sprungon' in Old English, and passed into Middle English as 'sprungen' until a later assimilation with the singular. (I doubt whether Housman had any of *that* in mind).

Those – and they must be many – who have never read any of the works of the self-styled 'Baron Corvo' have missed entry into an astonishing, isolated mind, and may thereby have missed very little; even his devotees often return with more pleasure to A. J. A. Symons's brilliant biography, *The Quest for Corvo*. But, for a vivid and eccentric

English style right out on a lonely and brittle limb, you should sample the novels, all laced with autobiography, of FREDERICK WILLIAM 'SERAFINO AUSTIN LEWIS MARY' ROLFE (1860–1913), who picked up four extra Christian names and a title as he went along. *Hubert's Arthur* (1909) imagines what would have happened if Prince Arthur had survived King John's enmity, and his reign is seen through the faithful eyes of Hubert de Burgh, his former gaoler (so they say) in a relationship made poignant by Shakespeare in *King John*. The first chapter opens as follows:

Because the day was very fair & the sun warm for the time of year, after my dinner I went to take the air, at ten of the glass, on the roof of the new watergate called Saint Thomas Beket his tower. There is a parcel of silly people, who believe the superstitious nonsense written by Mr Matthew (formerly of Paris,) averring that this tower is unsafe because it fell twice during its building; & they avoid it. But I sit here in the sun, day by day, for the confusion of such fatwits as well as for other reasons. The place is quiet, & apt for meditation, being high above the ant-heap of fortress & city. Here, an old man's eyes may follow the silvery river, as far as London Bridge, on the one hand; &, on the other, lose themselves far away over Lamehythe Marsh among the clean white pinnacles of the abbey & hall & palace of Westminster.

I had many matters for my meditation. There was a great crown-wearing this day in King William Redhair his hall at Westminster. And my lord the king was to do more awful & more difficult justice than ever before during his whole long reign. I had wished to stand in my place by his throne, where I always have stood in all his grave affairs. But his sweet grace, mindful of a very old earl's infirmities, bade me to take care of my health, for his sake & the kingdom's, sitting at home at my ease. Nevertheless, I thought of naught but the king's affairs throughout this sunny day. And, in the middle of the afternoon, Fulk the Flame, *vert, a heart between eight lyonceaux or*, came to me, hot from the crown-wearing. His fiery face was ashen-grey, & his manner quiet as cold cinders. 'Hubert, the king is dead:' says he.

So this is Rolfe's idea of an old aristocrat's speech and narrative style in the thirteenth century. Look for no rules, no skilful simulation of Middle English (or Anglo-Norman), no close recall of history; but you will find a many-faceted and multicoloured picture which might fascinate you. Shakespeare put the wrong kind of clock into *Julius Caesar*; Rolfe does better, but follows up with that old blunder of *Beket his* for 'Beketes' and so 'Beket's' (but at least he doesn't miscall him Thomas à Becket). That *parcel of silly people*, archaic without being thirteenth-century, shakes us, and prepares us for his wrapping the famous Matthew Paris up in an unfamiliar name; in a moment, he will do the same to Lambeth, and the old soldier, a man of sturdy views, will have shown his scorn at *fatwits* (though even *fatwitted* is no older than the sixteenth century), but the poetry of de Burgh's *silvery river* owes little to Middle English. We find *crown-wearing* an 'olde' form in the midst of all the common sense, but we have no substitute for it: this is one of the occasions when the King will actually wear his crown – to administer justice – and such verbal nouns have a dignity which we have found hard to explain. However, *this day* at once has a flavour, too; and *Redhair* for 'Rufus', along with the *his* mistake again, develops the rather sleepy old style into which the veteran has slipped. That the justice will be *awful* signifies only that it will inspire awe, not that it will be a mess. The impersonal *his sweet grace* is no older than *Her Majesty*; *bade* lingers unpronounceably even now in our formalities; and *sitting* pardonably 'dangles', since grammatically it *could* refer to the King; *naught* (without a *ne* to prelude it) is not as Middle English as Rolfe thinks. Then comes the thrilling arrival of a gentleman *and* his blazon (we no longer introduce our friends heraldically), along with hot-and-cold analogues of a type not contemporary with the events; but what he has to say is ageless, transcending the inversion and the sudden present tense of *says he*. Is all this typical Rolfe? I must reply that you never know what he is going to say next, or the language in which he will couch it.

Having considered four writers so wilful, we should remember that most Victorians were stirred far more by a traditional and dignified rhetoric, but also that this can be contrived and overdone, too. Fame and frequent quotation have attended the speech delivered in the Commons in 1855, against the Crimean War, by JOHN BRIGHT (1811–1889), of which this is the climax:

> The Angel of Death has been abroad throughout the land; you may almost hear the beating of his wings. There is no one, as when

the firstborn were slain of old, to sprinkle with blood the lintel and the two side-posts of our doors, that he may spare and pass on; he takes his victims from the castle of the noble, the mansion of the wealthy, and the cottage of the poor and the lowly, and it is on behalf of all these classes that I make this solemn appeal.

The requisite dignity is here, the cadence amounting to incantation, the apt use of the Passover rules as laid down in Exodus XII; Bright's audience would have been well educated in that original threat to the firstborn, but is not this politician blinding us somewhat with rhetoric, with orotund phrasing, with archaisms that will make the appeal less 'solemn' because less sincere? By 1855 *abroad* meant primarily 'away from Britain', and its combination with *throughout the land* was already awkward; does 'you may almost hear' imply possibility or capability? (we shall not burden it with the third meaning, permission); if the ominous figure 'has been' widespread, why can his wings be almost heard at present? (a frightening image, made pedestrian by the admission of 'almost'). In the second sentence, with what is 'as when the firstborn were slain' compared? – with there being no one, or (what is true but not proved here) with there being *someone*? The phrase 'slain of old' is in its two parts antiquated; *lintel* would be happier in the plural, since *doors* are specified; *that* is an archaism for *so that*. Purposely leaving out the uninteresting villas of the prosperous upper working class, Bright has to tarnish his poetry with the mention of 'classes'.

16 Novels Social and Anti-social

One of the earliest really disturbing novels was *Erewhon*, the anagram of 'nowhere', published in 1872 and attacking indiscriminately the most prized institutions of England. The author, SAMUEL BUTLER (1835–1902), produced less a novel than a treatise, a first-person fictional narrative with *his* extreme ideas about the truth of England framed in a satirical account of a newly discovered country. So the peculiarities of Erewhon are in turn stated, examined and coolly criticised, one of the oddest being the local belief that its people were all formerly living unborn, and foolishly contrived and conspired until they managed to get born into this sinful and disappointing world. A pen dipped in oil of vitriol might have seemed the obvious equipment to a coarser mind, but no surface passion or horror shows itself in the style that Butler sustains:

> They feel this so strongly that they are resolved to shift the blame on to other shoulders; and have fashioned a long mythology as to the world in which the unborn people live, and what they do, and the arts and machinations to which they have recourse in order to get themselves into our own world. But of this more anon; what I would relate here is their manner of dealing with those who do come.
>
> It is a distinguishing peculiarity of the Erewhonians that when they profess themselves to be quite certain about any matter, and avow it as a base on which they are to build a system of practice, they seldom quite believe in it. If they smell a rat about the precincts of a cherished institution, they will always stop their noses to it if they can.
>
> This is what most of them did in this matter of the unborn, for I

cannot (and never could) think that they seriously believed in their mythology concerning pre-existence; they did and they did not; they did not know themselves what they believed; all they did know was that it was a disease not to believe as they did. The only thing of which they were quite sure was that it was the pestering of the unborn [ambiguous: are they pestering or being pestered?] which caused them to be brought into this world, and that they would not have been here if they would have [vulgar for 'if they had'] only let peaceable people alone.

It would be hard to disprove this position, and they might have a good case if they would only leave it as it stands. But this they will not do; they must have assurance doubly sure; they must have the written word of the child itself as soon as it is born, giving the parents indemnity from all responsibility on the score of its birth, and asserting its own pre-existence.

This has a peculiarly rancid style; but, I suppose, when you think everyone else is in the wrong – churchmen, statesmen, parents, the mercantile, the traditional and the respectable – you will imperiously adopt the condescending and bored simplicity of this endless ground-clearing. That the information is nonsense, that interest in it and serious discussion of it are bound to be nonsense as well, keeps the prose uninspired and toneless; the only figures of speech are legal ('system of practice', 'a good case', 'indemnity') or ugly and hackneyed ('other shoulders', 'smell a rat', 'stop their noses', 'assurance doubly sure'); a pointless and incorrect archaism occurs – 'anon' – and the parenthesis '(and never could)' is ambiguous, with its choice of meanings 'I was never able' or 'I would never be able'. Butler writes here as if not moving his teeth; a monotonous sequence of restrained sarcasm (the sarcasm is in the apparent restraint) is conveyed by a string of monosyllables that reach their depth with the frequent help of the barren idioms *do* and *did*, as in 'all they did know was that it was a disease not to believe as they did' – is this 'as they *did*' or 'as *they* did'?

JOSEPH CONRAD (1857–1924) lets us hear *Heart of Darkness* (1902) only at several removes: it is told, in quotation marks throughout, by the troubled and over-experienced sailor Marlow, and the author – himself of course a trained skipper with twenty years at sea – guesses it to be one of Marlow's 'inconclusive experiences', and may be wrong (since he makes himself one of the audience) in thus prejudging the tale. It reaches us through impressions or realities of horror, we do not know which, but before the feverish incidents in the jungle begin we meet a figure who imparts a welcome (and misleading) cool shade:

> 'When near the buildings I met a white man, in such an unexpected elegance of get-up that in the first moment I took him for a sort of vision. I saw a high starched collar, white cuffs, a light alpaca jacket, snowy trousers, a clean necktie, and varnished boots. No hat. Hair parted, brushed, oiled, under a green-lined parasol held in a big white hand. He was amazing, and had a pen-holder behind his ear.
>
> 'I shook hands with this miracle, and I learned he was the Company's chief accountant, and that all the book-keeping was done at this station. He had come out for a moment, he said, "to get a breath of fresh air." The expression sounded wonderfully odd, with its suggestion of sedentary desk-life. I wouldn't have mentioned the fellow to you at all, only it was from his lips that I first heard the name of the man who is so indissolubly connected with the memories of that time. Moreover, I respected the fellow. Yes; I respected his collars, his vast cuffs, his brushed hair. His appearance was certainly that of a hairdresser's dummy; but in the great demoralisation of the land he kept up his appearance. That's backbone. His starched collars and got-up shirt-fronts were achievements of character.'

The method here is itemisation, not impressionism. We see him with clarity, and the asyntactical 'No hat.' wastes no time. His elegance and whiteness make him 'amazing' (no other particular qualities have yet been mentioned), and the extra touch to this first sight is the clerkly pen in his ear. Suddenly he becomes a 'miracle', whose phrasing is 'wonderfully odd', yet (apologetically) he's not worth mentioning save for the information he gave; still, Marlow 'respected' him (though 'fellow' isn't a very kind word). The respect proves to be for some insignificant things – collars, cuffs, pomaded hair. The prose, a strong man's narrative spoken to strong men, has temporarily a neatness and precision that enact the well-kept accounts of this 'sort of vision', and Conrad, the Pole whose mastery of both formal and colloquial English is so admirable, even allows him the traditional British quality of 'backbone', and will praise the 'apple-pie order' of his books.

But the river narrows, the jungle closes in, and as if in deliberate contrast a plucky little figure presents himself – the Russian, 'son of an arch-priest . . . Government of Tambov':

'As I manoeuvred to get alongside, I was asking myself, "What does this fellow look like?" Suddenly I got it. He looked like a harlequin. His clothes had been made of some stuff that was brown holland probably, but it was covered with patches all over, with bright patches, blue, red, and yellow – patches on the back, patches on the front, patches on elbows, on knees; coloured binding round his jacket, scarlet edging at the bottom of his trousers; and the sunshine made him look extremely gay and wonderfully neat withal, because you could see how beautifully all this patching had been done. A beardless, boyish face, very fair, no features to speak of, nose peeling, little blue eyes, smiles and frowns chasing each other over that open countenance like sunshine and shadow on a wind-swept plain.'

There is a kind of madness here, and a mystery of identity, but they are still presented in items, though the simile of a wind-swept plain far different from the jungle is needed. But when they have met and smoked and talked, there is time for implications, and these require a flurry of adjectives – long Latinate ones – and abstract nouns:

'I looked at him, lost in astonishment. There he was before me, in motley, as though he had absconded from a troupe of mimes, enthusiastic, fabulous. His very existence was improbable, inexplicable, and altogether bewildering. He was an insoluble problem. It was inconceivable how he had existed, how he had succeeded in getting so far, how he had managed to remain – why he did not instantly disappear. "I went a little farther," he said, "then still a little farther – till I had gone so far that I don't know how I'll ever get back. Never mind. Plenty time. I can manage. You take Kurtz away quick – quick – I tell you." The glamour of youth enveloped his parti-coloured rags, his destitution, his loneliness, the essential desolation of his futile wanderings. For months – for years – his life hadn't been worth a day's purchase; and there he was gallantly, thoughtlessly alive, to all appearances indestructible solely by the virtue of his few years and of his unreflecting audacity. I was seduced into something like admiration – like envy. Glamour urged him on.'

The speculations here are full of prickly words – *fabulous, improbable, inexplicable, insoluble, inconceivable, manage* (*manage* to remain, or just *manage*), *destitution, loneliness, desolation, futile*. Marlow sees in him the 'absolutely pure, uncalculating, unpractical spirit of adventure', a 'modest and clear flame'. Yet it remains hard to believe in Harlequin, and subsequent disclosures less to his credit will make it harder or easier according to our grasp of some pretty huge issues. Perhaps the froth of long words in this last passage is meant to convey Marlow's inadequacy – he is getting things wrong, and in the impenetrable darkness that surrounds Kurtz the counting and the cataloguing have to stop.

Mere parody can be very skilful and very salutary, though at its worst it requires only malicious observation of a writer's style or obsessions. When JAMES JOYCE (1882–1941) applied its methods in the Nausicaa episode of *Ulysses*, his butt was the sentimental novelette; Homer's Nausicaa story was of a staunch young princess who loved in vain but accepted her emptied future with sense and dignity, and we see how glaringly unworthy was Joyce's model, and how the sweetness and girlishness and goo, in hackneyed and unmeant phrases, are perverted into conveying a very different society from that of the novels of Ethel M. Dell or Charles Garvice. The sun is setting on Dublin Bay and 'last but not least' on a church (where the service is going to be parodied and misused as well):

> The three girl friends were seated on the rocks, enjoying the evening scene and the air which was fresh but not too chilly. Many a time and oft were they wont to come there to that favourite nook to have a cosy chat beside the sparkling waves and discuss matters feminine, Cissy Caffrey and Edy Boardman with the baby in the pushcar and Tommy and Jacky Caffrey, two little curly-headed boys, dressed in sailor suits with caps to match and the name H.M.S. Belleisle printed on both. For Tommy and Jacky Caffrey were twins, scarce four years old and very noisy and spoiled twins

sometimes but for all that darling little fellows with bright merry faces and endearing ways about them. They were dabbling in the sand with their spades and buckets, building castles as children do, or playing with their big coloured ball, happy as the day was long. And Edy Boardman was rocking the chubby baby to and fro in the pushcar while that young gentleman fairly chuckled with delight. He was but eleven months and nine days old and, though still a tiny toddler, was just beginning to lisp his first babyish words. Cissy Caffrey bent over him to tease his fat little plucks and the dainty dimple in his chin. . . . . . .

Cissy Caffrey cuddled the wee chap for she was awfully fond of children, so patient with little sufferers and Tommy Caffrey could never be got to take his castor oil unless it was Cissy Caffrey that held his nose and promised him the scatty heel of the loaf of brown bread with golden syrup on. What a persuasive power that girl had! But to be sure baby was as good as gold, a perfect little dote in his new fancy bib. None of your spoilt beauties, Flora MacFlimsy sort, was Cissy Caffrey. A truerhearted lass never drew the breath of life, always with a laugh in her gipsylike eyes and a frolicsome word on her cherryripe red lips, a girl lovable in the extreme.

The string of cliches, the antiquated ('Many a time and oft were they wont') in uneasy neighbourhood with the modern ('cosy chat', 'matters feminine'), will soon suggest that there is little genuine about this gaggle of girls; the temporary narrator is suddenly a garrulous Agony Column stylist, whose headlong lack of punctuation is just right for the bits of reminiscence which it sweeps into its burbling course. After a very discreet mention of little Tommy's underpants as 'unmentionables', and the arrangements for his toilet, we are back in the pure air surrounding the third girl:

Gerty MacDowell who was seated near her companions, lost in thought, gazing far away into the distance, was in very truth as fair a specimen of winsome Irish girlhood as one could wish to see. She was pronounced beautiful by all who knew her though, as folks often said, she was more a Giltrap than a MacDowell. Her figure was slight and graceful, inclining even to fragility but those iron jelloids she had been taking of late had done her a world of good much better than the Widow Welch's female pills and she was much better of those discharges she used to get and that tired feeling. The waxen pallor of her face was almost spiritual in its ivorylike purity though her rosebud mouth was a genuine Cupid's bow, Greekly perfect. Her hands were of finely veined alabaster with tapering fingers and as white as lemon juice and queen of ointments could make them though it was not true that she used to wear kid gloves in bed or take a milk footbath either. Bertha Supple told that once to Edy Boardman, a deliberate lie, when she was black out at daggers drawn with Gerty (the girl chums had of course their little tiffs from time to time like the rest of mortals) and she told her not let on whatever she did that it was her that told her or she'd never speak to her again. No. Honour where honour is due.

The intrusions of clinical realism and petty squabbles, treated on an equal footing with this cloying prose, are further proof that there is nothing romantic about these girls, although

Gerty's crowning glory was her wealth of wonderful hair. It was dark brown with a natural wave in it. She had cut it that very morning on account of the new moon and it nestled about her pretty head in a profusion of luxuriant clusters and pared her nails too, Thursday for wealth. And just now at Edy's words as a telltale flush, delicate as the faintest rosebloom, crept into her cheeks she looked so lovely in her sweet girlish shyness that of a surety God's fair land of Ireland did not hold her equal.

The rambling style bothers more about expressions like 'crowning glory', 'telltale flush' and 'of a surety' than about proper syntax, and apparently what pared her nails was her hair, and not Gerty. She has not yet started behaving like a calculating minx, and the statement that her 'languid queenly *hauteur*' was evidenced in her 'higharched instep' is an evasion of the fact that she had a lame leg, on which she hobbles out of a fundamentally sordid story.

JOHN GALSWORTHY (1867–1933) has of late received a great boost of reputation by what felt to many like an incessant television serial, *The Forsyte Saga*. There are 1,104 pages of it in the many Heinemann reprints from 1922 on. As social history, as scrutiny of character, as reproducing the conversation of middle-class people, and for many qualities expected of a novel, it still looks praiseworthy to many, but its prose style grows tired and careless off and on. When Jolyon calls on Irene (p. 508 of the Heinemann edition),

> The effect of a settled if very modest income was at once apparent to him remembering the threadbare refinement in that tiny flat eight years ago when he announced her good fortune. Everything was now fresh, dainty, and smelled of flowers. The general effect was silvery with touches of black, hydrangea colour, and gold. 'A woman of great taste', he thought. Time had dealt gently with Jolyon, for he was a Forsyte. But with Irene time hardly seemed to deal at all – or such was his impression. She appeared to him not a day older, standing there in mole-coloured velvet corduroy, with soft dark eyes and dark gold hair, with outstretched hand and a little smile.

This starts with an improper *if*: the truth of the income's being modest in no way affects its being settled, but the wording suggests that if it *wasn't* modest then it was unsettled; why not just *though very modest* or *but very modest*? The word *remembering* is vague to this extent, that it can mean 'considering' or 'in view of'; *when he remembered* would make it quite clear that *we* are not being called on to remember the incident eight years ago. In the second sentence Galsworthy forgets that, in two statements joined by *and*, any little catalogue must have its own *and* as well; so this should read: 'Everything was now fresh *and* dainty, and smelled of flowers'. Jolyon's assessment of Irene is made to sound very gingerly: 'Time hardly seemed' to touch her – or at least he got that 'impression. She appeared to him . . .'. That *hardly seemed* is downright bad; *seemed hardly* is a little better, but – as so often with this dangerous word – is the seeming just another reality concealed? Look under the make-up and you'll find the truth? In the last sentence, who was *standing*? – grammatically it could agree with *him* as much as with *She*, and he would look quite natty in that *mole-coloured velvet corduroy*. A novel of 1,104 pages will contain a lot of automatic writing, and I suppose few of the general public will find this chunk of it as offensive as *I* do.

But he wrote plays as well, and earnest ones at that, and their audiences will have demanded authentic conversation. Sometimes they got it: the little-known *A Bit o'Love* is conducted half in Devon dialect and partly in the gentle speech of a broken-hearted curate, but

Escape (1926), once popular with amateurs despite its twelve different scenes, has some of the most stilted wording of the stage of the 1920s. A Dartmoor prisoner has escaped, and is being sought near the cottage of two genteel sisters, Grace ('about forty-seven') and Dora ('much younger'), who is in 'hunting togs' and just returned.

> DORA: There's such a glow on the Cleave, Grace. Most lovely red. We killed. Everybody was looking out for that escaped convict.
> GRACE: Did you see him?
> DORA: No, thank goodness. Poor hunted wretch!
> GRACE: If you think hunted things are poor, why do you go hunting?
> DORA: Foxes hunt and expect to be hunted.
> GRACE: So do convicts. Sympathy's wasted on them. Tea, Dora.
> DORA: This isn't a common convict. It's that Captain Denant, you remember –
> GRACE: Oh! – not likely to forget the row we had about his case. Well! it served him right!
> DORA: For a good woman, Grace, you know – you're awfully hard.
> GRACE: Tea-cake, please. I like consistency.

And so on. As the script for a formal abbreviated debate, or the tit-for-tat *stichomythia* of a Greek play, it will serve; but from the hard lady's mocking name, Grace, and her callous request for that most respectable of foods, tea-cake, we know that we are in for a formula, and that they will behave exactly as they do when the convict enters through the French windows – and more so, because he is such a ripping decent chap who can converse in single pithy lines just as *they* can. Stage conversation has coarsened in the last sixty years; you never know what awful things they'll say next – but this pair have gone through their parts before.

There is so much 'fine writing' in the novels of JOHN COWPER POWYS (1872–1963) that it is easy to spot the inconsistency, the over-written phrases, the tedious parallelism of epithet *plus* noun, which so often unworthily accompany the big issues of evil and death and matter and their opposites. A novel with some especially nasty features, *Wolf Solent* (1929), works up to what is intended, after six hundred pages, to be a great self-realisation, and near this climax a

typical paragraph contains this Powys mixture of petty nonchalance
and apocalypse:

> As they crossed the fields towards the cemetery, Wolf visualized the
> journey of those two old men that night. In some queer way he felt
> as if Carfax were a competent actor, naturally assuming the precise
> role in which he himself had failed! Carfax would hear that imbecile
> youth cry out 'Longborne Port!' and rattle the milk-cans on that
> little, deserted platform! Carfax would see the tower of Basingstoke
> Church. Carfax would see that placid-grazing cow. Carfax would
> observe, crossing the same coloured picture of Weymouth Bay, the
> same blue bottle fly . . . or his exact representative . . . in the
> whirligig of chance!

This is incredibly slack. Where does *that night* belong? – one has to
read and think back to determine that it refers to a slightly later
journey, not to the time when Wolf is thinking. Is *he* thinking *In some
queer way*, or is this the limit of Carfax's histrionic powers? – and *felt as
if* is babble for 'felt that', and not to be encouraged in stylists. Who is
naturally assuming? – we see quickly, but not immediately as we should,
that it is Carfax; and *he himself* should then refer to Carfax, the subject
of the parenthesis – but it doesn't. Next, Carfax is going to hear the
young porter and then, apparently, rattle the milk-cans; Powys is
forgetting that *would . . . rattle* is grammatically as feasible as the
twinning of *cry* and *rattle*. The *placid-grazing* cow has some novelty
'over and above' (as we strangely say) mere 'placid, grazing' or
'placid grazing', but it is a novelty easily achieved and not to be too
often repeated. And what's Carfax doing crossing a picture of
Weymouth Bay? There are many ways of writing badly, and Powys
has hit on a few of them here; some of us may deprecate mixed
metaphors, but they are a stylistic matter and can be correct
grammatically, whereas these displacements of phrases clog and
delay every sentence in which they occur. No highly-publicised
author will be guilty of wrong inflexions; but, unsheltered by their
publishers, scholars have said in my hearing 'I was sat', 'I was
laid/laying', and 'If I'd've known'. Pedants have made a great fuss
about the 'wrong' use of *will* for the 1st person, which they assert
should be *shall*; there is no warrant for this save recent use, and it
strikes me as utter folly to insist on *I shall, you will, he will, we shall, they
will*, reversing the *sh-* and *w-* for the emphatic forms. But Powys's

prime error is that, lost in the mazes of pretentiousness and grotesque characterisation, he strings together his visionary phrases with little regard for the whole syntactical structure.

E. M. FORSTER (1879–1970) thought that his best novel was *The Longest Journey* (1907), and it is not hard to agree, though some have found its sudden deaths astonishing, and their dismissal callous. It is interesting to see how they are managed. The first victim is a gorgeous brute and bully, 'intellectually a prude' . . . 'like most men who are rather animals'; his current interests are the Army, football, and a pretty possessive love soon to be crowned by marriage.

> Gerald died that afternoon. He was broken up in the football match. Rickie [the wan hero] and Mr Pembroke were on the ground when the accident took place. It was no good torturing him by a drive to the hospital, and he was merely carried to the little pavilion and laid upon the floor. A doctor came, and so did a clergyman, but it seemed better to leave him for the last few minutes with Agnes, who had ridden down on her bicycle.
>
> It was a strange lamentable interview. The girl was so accustomed to health, that for a time she could not understand. It must be a joke that he chose to lie there in the dust, with a rug over him, and his knees bent up towards his chin. His arms were as she knew them, and their admirable muscles showed clear and clean beneath the jersey. The face, too, though a little flushed, was uninjured: it must be some curious joke.

After a desultory conversation, in which his loss of sight accompanies his loss of faith, the sadistic snob dies in her arms: 'Only this time her grasp was the stronger'. The neat narrative, which changes the whole course of the novel one-sixth the way through, clearly hints that he got what he deserved. The unsporty Forster curiously says *football match* where we would just say *match*; Gerald sounds like the worst type of rugby player, but his creator doesn't specify.

Rickie's mother dies with almost as little warning; recently widowed (to her great benefit), and with plans for a happy move into the country, she urges her son to put on his greatcoat to go out – the weather being raw; he is devoted to her, but he is now all of fifteen, and twice repudiates the idea before saying:

'Oh, I shan't catch cold. I do wish you wouldn't keep on bothering'.

He did not catch cold, but while he was out his mother died. She only survived her husband eleven days, a coincidence which was recorded on their tombstone. [Most of us would prefer 'only eleven days'] . . . About the greatcoat he did not tell them, for he could not have spoken of it without tears.

This is masterly; Rickie is reproducing every scrap of that last conversation, its petty circumstances, and his own remembered guilt, and the wording is deathly plain. But towards the end of the novel we are let into a terrible secret: a love-child, believed to belong to Rickie's frightful father, is *hers*. She was briefly rescued from her loveless marriage by a wholesome young farmer; they honeymooned in Sweden, where he disobligingly

had been drowned. Mrs Elliott described how they had gone swimming, and how, 'since he had always lived inland', the great waves had tired him. They had raced for the open sea . . . .

'I heard him call', she continued, 'but I thought he was laughing. When I turned, it was too late. He put his hands behind his back and sank. For [but *do* we commonly use 'For' rather than 'Because'?] he would only have drowned me with him. I should have done the same'. [An awkward instance of 'should' – does she mean 'Had I been in his situation, I would/should have done the same' or 'That's what *I* ought to have done'?]

Before the end, it is Rickie's turn. His drunken half-brother has strayed on to the railway line by night, and is lying on the rails as the slow goods train approaches:

Wearily he did a man's duty. There was time to raise him up and push him into safety. It is also a man's duty to save his own life, and therefore he tried. The train went over his knees. He died up in Cadover . . .

Well, these four sudden deaths have their ghoulish side, but there is no mistaking the tragic depth of Rickie's feelings at that lowest point in his fortunes when his job and marriage and identity are all revealed as a sham, when his baby, as lame as himself, is dead, and he has just dreamed of his mother 'crying quite distinctly in the darkened room':

He lit a candle, and the room was empty. Then, hurrying to the window, he saw above mean houses the frosty glories of Orion.

Henceforward he deteriorates. Let those who censure him suggest what he should do. He has lost the work that he loved, his friends, and his child. He remained conscientious and decent, but the spiritual part of him proceeded towards ruin.

The excellence of this is not ascribable to any special technique; the central portion in the present tense is urgent, and a warning not to judge an imperfect character; Orion occurs elsewhere – just before Rickie's death, as if the constellation were for Forster the substitute for a religious symbol; and the cold scene, and the following analysis of human behaviour, well enact the coldness of Rickie's emptied heart.

Wielding a style almost as capricious as Rolfe's, and like him a convert to Roman Catholicism, RONALD FIRBANK (1886–1926) has been lavishly called the 'first and almost the only Impressionist in English fiction'. Well, even if this is so, it certainly isn't achieved by linguistic tricks – a shifting tense-pattern, or violations of syntax, or antiquated spellings, or staccato wording which could look impressionistic. *Valmouth* (1919), potty yet skilful – 'You wouldn't've known there'd been a war on', as they say, – plunges straight in at the beginning of Chapter I:

Day was drooping on a fine evening in March as a brown barouche passed through the wrought-iron gates at Hare-Hatch House on to the open highway.

Beneath the crepuscular, tinted sky the countryside stretched away, interspersed with hamlets, meads and woods, towards low, loosely engirdling hills, that rose up against the far horizon with a fine monastic roll.

Although it was but the third month of the year, yet, from a singular softness of the air, already the trees were in full, fresh leaf. Along the hedgerows hawthorns were in bloom, while the many wild flowers by the roadside scented in fitful whiffs an invigorating, caressing breeze.

Seated immediately behind the coachman in the shell-like carriage was a lady no longer young. Her fragile features, long and pointed, were swathed, quasi-biblically, in a striped Damascus shawl that looked Byzantine, at either side of which escaped a wisp of red, crimped hair. . . . Facing the ladies a biretta'd priest appeared to be perusing a little, fat, black, greasy book of prayers. . . . .

The first sentence uses, not indiscreetly, the native gift of alliteration: two *d*s, and two *b*s, and in some haste four *h*s; this will recur in the third little paragraph, with the pretty words *singular, softness, full, fresh, hedgerows, hawthorns*; indeed, one senses that this is a gentle mockery of fine writing, using clichés like *caressing* and sentimentalities like *but the third month* for 'only March'. We are offered a number of different 'impressions'; *crepuscular* takes us absurdly back to a French lyric, *meads* to the eighteenth century, *monastic* to the religiosity from which all the pampered characters suffer. The coyly dated female magnate, *fragile* yet proving to have a great gusto for living, looks Damascene (or is it Byzantine?), and dyes her hair red. The priest is *biretta'd* (again, why not *birettaed*?) and has a greasy prayer-book. There is another dire woman in the carriage; a minute later, we have received the 'impression' that these three are not very fond of one another. And, as with Rolfe, the oddity and invention are endless.

17 Critical and Devotional Prose

The poetic style of T. S. ELIOT (1888–1965) has so often been thanked and praised for its liberative power, its diction that none had ever used before, and its upsetting *mots justes*, that it should be possible to find it in his prose, especially in that critical prose concerned with other poets; but the search proves (rather unreasonably) disappointing – or proves that Eliot kept the media apart, save in the prosy idioms of his later verse plays. ('I had no idea it was in poetry' was the kind of remark one heard in the foyer afterwards). His important and generous essay on Milton in *Essays and Studies* (1936) begins with a flawed passage which would not normally lure me on:

> While it must be admitted that Milton is a very great poet indeed, it is something of a puzzle to decide in what his greatness consists. On analysis, the marks against him appear both more numerous and more significant than the marks to his credit. As a man, he is antipathetic. Either from the moralist's point of view, or from the theologian's point of view, or from the psychologist's point of view, or from that of the political philosopher, or judging by the ordinary standards of likeableness in human beings, Milton is unsatisfactory. The doubts which I have to express about him are more serious than these. His greatness as a poet has been sufficiently celebrated, though I think largely for the wrong reasons, and without the proper reservations. His misdeeds as a poet have been called attention to, as by Mr Ezra Pound, but usually in passing.

From the very first word, I feel hostile to some of this. *While* truly means 'so long as', 'only so long as'; its sense of concurrency is strong, and its extra use as 'though' overburdens it. A passive verb, *it must be admitted*, follows at once, and the fewer of these the better; a person, a mind, is behind them, and the mere passivity and abstraction are bloodless. Then *something of a puzzle* is untrue, without being imaginative; and what exactly does *On analysis* mean here? – are the marks analysed, or is it 'on our making a general analysis'? – and *appear* is as unsafe as 'seem'; do the marks 'only appear' so, but inaccurately? The idea of giving Milton marks is not attractive, and the repetition of the word gives warning of the triple occurrence of *point of view* which will follow. Now comes a sentence meant to act as a hinge, of a mere six words; *antipathetic* is 'daringly' used without its normal adjunct 'to', but at the price that we remain unsure whether Milton dislikes us or we dislike Milton. The threefold *point of view* is ugly, and why the coyness about using a fourth and last, with a *that of* instead? Are the *standards* in the human beings, or in the likeableness? (after all, beings wield standards which are *in* them, and good qualities are *in* them also). The next sentence, cold and trenchant, is yet ambiguous; the doubts are more serious than these *what*? – points of view, or stirrings of dissatisfaction? In the next sentence, *though I think largely for the wrong reasons* suggests an absurd admission that 'my thought processes are touched off irrationally', and the easy solution, a comma on either side of *I think*, must of course be applied. The passives have started again: *greatness . . . has been . . . celebrated, misdeeds . . . have been called attention to* – a hideous phrase; and *as* in *as by Mr Ezra Pound* is an insufficient signal for 'for instance' – it suggests that all such comment was in imitation of Pound. It is as well that we have come to the end of the passage; I shall be accused of iconoclasm or puerile carping, but here a great critic is starting an influential essay, and his modesty and timidity at this are making his hand shake.

After four hundred years of a Biblical and liturgical English unmatched by any other language and apparently irreplaceable (but see, alas, below) C.S. LEWIS (1898–1963) had to hit on the idiom which a senior devil might use for the opposite purpose. From his place in the lowerarchy, Screwtape wrote *The Screwtape Letters* (London: Geoffrey Bles, 1942) to his nephew Wormwood, who had an assignment on earth. Lewis was devout and scholarly, and a brilliant stylist – with a sense of humour that saved him from any pomposity; wisely, he let Screwtape compose his arguments against the Enemy

(God) in a clear, fastidious style. Here, he explains to the young fiend a large issue concerning the diabolical way with mortals:

> Our business is to get them away from the eternal, and from the Present. With this in view, we sometimes tempt a human (say a widow or a scholar) to live in the Past. But this is of limited value, for they have some real knowledge of the Past and it has a determinate nature and, to that extent, resembles Eternity. It is far better to make them live in the Future. Biological necessity makes all their passions point in that direction already, so that thought about the Future inflames hope and fear. Also, it is unknown to them, so that in making them think about it we make them think of unrealities. In a word, the Future is, of all things, the thing *least like* eternity. It is the most completely temporal part of time – for the Past is frozen and no longer flows, and the Present is all lit up with eternal rays. Hence the encouragement we have given to all those schemes of thought such as Creative Evolution, Scientific Humanism, or Communism, which fix men's affections on the Future, on the very core of temporality. Hence nearly all vices are rooted in the future. Gratitude looks to the past and love to the present; fear, avarice, lust, and ambition look ahead.

This wit and neatness, this intellectual coolness from within the flames of Hell, are sustained throughout the book; no phrase is illogical or obscure, or awkward to hear aloud. Why could this style, in which the foiled Screwtape rises in the last chapter to an unwitting piece of strong evangelism, not colour the theology of a later generation? I ignore the typical theological writings of today: their heresies, their cant, their huge words, their attack on tradition and the substitution of a void; the various new Bibles are comprehensible, though that is no excuse for making the King James Bible out of date. But why did the powers that be (a phrase from that pioneer Bible translator, Tyndale) not only formulate, but foist on the Church of England, that debased form of the Book of Common Prayer called the Alternative Service Book (1980)?

The Prayer Book of 1662, which had for so long looked timeless, was of course, from its human sources, not a perfect document, though its many adherents can be forgiven for thinking it was. We wriggled slightly in the Second Collect at Evening Prayer, when the parallel of 'that both' with 'and also that' involved us in the misleading phrase 'both our hearts'; we knew that there were some preposterous phrases in the version (substantially Coverdale's) of the Psalter – unsingable and incomprehensible, like Psalm xii 5, 'Now for the comfortless trouble's sake of the needy'; and the sources of the little errors and inconsistencies are well set out by Stella Brook in *The Language of the Book of Common Prayer* (London: Andre Deutsch, 1965). The modest 'additions and deviations' proposed in 1928 were never authorised, though some of them have been used ever since; but despite the threats from more casual Bibles, the English of the Church remained sweet and strong, cadenced not colloquial, traditional not topical, until the divisive forms of service licensed under the terms of the Prayer Book (Alternative and Other Services) Measure 1965 besotted so many of the bishops and ecclesiastical bureaucrats that the people found their familiar Book supplanted. An eminent edition of the *PN Review*, No. 13 of 1979, guest-edited by Professor David Martin, was effectively ignored by the General Synod, and in 1980 'the wellsprings of expressive power' (as the *Review* called the work of 1611 and 1662) were choked by the issue of the fat book of Alternatives. Its far more hesitant attitude to sin, its trendy *you/you/your* for *thou/thee/thy*, its avoidance of awe whenever information to God can be substituted, are theological matters; its stylistic faults are for everyone's discomfort.

But even a little easy passage, always communicable, can be put through pointless adventures to groom it for the 1980s. Let the Collect at the outset of Holy Communion serve as an example not so much painful as irritating in its futile interference with warm, cadenced wording. The 1662 Book reads:

> Almighty God, unto whom all hearts be open, all desires known, and from no secrets are hid: Cleanse the thoughts of our hearts by the inspiration of thy Holy Spirit, that we may perfectly love thee, and worthily magnify thy holy Name; through Christ our Lord. *Amen.*

Now those who pretended that liturgical English was hard could have found material for their argument here: how their fingers must have itched to 'correct' the archaic *unto* to *to* and *be* to *are*, to insert an 'and' after *open* (since *hearts* and *desires* form their own little catalogue), to modernise the past participle to *hidden*, open out the *that* of purpose to *so that*, put an up-to-date word for *magnify*, which is now altogether too scientific, and of course abolish *thee* and *thy*. The result in Series 3 was set out as verse (but not really):

> Almighty God,
> to whom all hearts are open,
> all desires known,
> and from whom no secrets are hid:
> cleanse the thoughts of our hearts
> by the inspiration of your Holy Spirit,
> that we may perfectly love you,
> and worthily magnify your holy Name;
> through Christ our Lord. Amen.

So four of the objectionable old forms are left untouched – the missing *and*, the archaic *hid*, the mere *that* for *so that*, and *magnify*. What kind of language is this, and how will the final draft of 1980 emerge? Like this:

> Almighty God,
> to whom all hearts are open,
> all desires known,
> and from whom no secrets are hidden:
> cleanse the thoughts of our hearts
> by the inspiration of your Holy Spirit,
> that we may perfectly love you,
> and worthily magnify your holy name;
> through Christ our Lord. Amen.

Only *hid* has been 'corrected' (to the compilers' taste); the rest, the faulty *and* and *that* and *magnify*, archaic and therefore anomalous in this liberated book, plod on, with the subtle addition that the reverence due to the Name of God is withdrawn in the spelling *name*.

18 Humour, Mature and Childlike

It is likely that some of the brightest examples of linguistic resource will be found in humorous verse; but such verse is so often mainly facetious that it cannot stand by the classics, or the earnestly intended classics, that I have mostly used. This is where so many readers find OGDEN NASH (1902–1971) of merit; he is genuinely observant of what is abidingly and harmlessly funny, he is not sick or bitter, he uses for uproarious ends the methods of poetry, the vision and the vicissitudes of the poetic life. The most famous tools in his equipment are his elaborate multiple rhymes and, held together by them, his freely longwinded and irregular couplets; but he can conform, with a much primmer metric, as in 'Tableau at Twilight' in *Versus* (London: J. M. Dent, 1949 and subsequently):

I sit in the dusk. I am all alone.
Enter a child and an ice-cream cone.

A parent is easily beguiled
By sight of this coniferous child.

The friendly embers warmer gleam,
The cone begins to drip ice cream.

Cones are composed of many a vitamin.
My lap is not the place to bitamin.

Although my raiment is not chinchilla,
I flinch to see it become vanilla.

Coniferous child, when vanilla melts
I'd rather it melted somewhere else.

Exit child with remains of cone.
I sit in the dusk. I am all alone,

Muttering spells like an angry Druid,
Alone, in the dusk, with the cleaning fluid.

This is American humour, but it is wholly British, too. Its methods
are quite straightforward. Everything is in the present tense, so there
is immediacy as of a great drama. There are two statements in the first
line, then a stage-direction; a quaint one, because the child isn't 'with'
the ice-cream cornet (as we British prefer to say) – the delicacy enters
of itself. The second couplet is a nice loving generalisation, but it
becomes sharply particularised in that fine misuse of *coniferous*, which
you and I know is used of trees that bear cones. The fifth line lulls us
with its warm poetic jargon, but warmth doesn't team with ice-cream
(which he cannot here spell with a hyphen, as before; it has to be a
phrase of two equal stresses). Next, a mirthful rhyme on three
syllables, involving the serious subjects of vitamins and of a loving
father trying hard to feel cross – though I would not wish to adopt the
verb-pronoun-preposition *bitamin*; and the next couplet plays with the
cacophony of *chinchilla . . . flinch*. After two rich rhymes, *melts* and *else*
are no doubt intentionally 'wrong'; the plea to the child is the nearest
it gets to a rebuke, and is very apologetic. Maintaining the itemising
present tense to the very end, the poet sits alone poetically, but angry,
now that the child need not suffer from the anger; and then, in the
poetic dusk, the whole picture goes beautifully wrong – he's dabbing
on cleaning fluid. It would obviously be great fun to draw on other
humorous writers of this genial man's ability; it would also be
relevant.

For the poor who, in the absense of a rich cultural background, must
imaginatively live off the land and double every visual impression by
keen-eyed and also whimsical analogies, that 'manipulator of words',
DYLAN THOMAS (1914–1953), is a good model. In his prose story,
The Outing, 25 prettily illustrated pages in the J. M. Dent edition of
1971, he is an ordinary little boy 'staying . . . with' a shrew aunt and a
rogue uncle, and pretty content. The men take him on their
charabanc outing, and we know that Thomas will not be able to resist
putting into the urchin's mind a poet's impish imagination; we can
excuse this by seeing it as impressions recollected in maturity.

The charabanc pulled up outside the Mountain Sheep, a small, unhappy public-house with a thatched roof like a wig with ringworm. From a flagpole by the Gents fluttered the flag of Siam. I knew it was the flag of Siam because of cigarette cards. The landlord stood at the door to welcome us, simpering like a wolf. He was a long, lean, black-fanged man with a greased love-curl and pouncing eyes. 'What a beautiful August day!' he said, and touched his love-curl with a claw. That was the way he must have welcomed the Mountain Sheep before he ate it, I said to myself. The members rushed out, bleating, and into the bar.

Now this is not the authentic streaming of a child's consciousness, though a strongly imaginative child might be gripped by his vision of a wolf, whereafter the fangs, the 'pouncing' eyes, the claw, the deceived sheep and the bleating flock of customers follow naturally. A child who has seen a wig and (as was common in rough schools in the 1920s) ringworm, *might* put the two together at sight of a thatch, and the proud quoting of the authority of cigarette cards is altogether childlike. They pub-crawl on, the little nobody excluded from the mysteries, but quite himself as he snuggles up against one of his uncle's bellies and collects the names of the inns. 'Closing time meant nothing' to them:

> Behind locked doors, they hymned and rumpused all the beautiful afternoon. And, when a policeman entered the Druid's Tap by the back door, and found them all choral with beer, 'Sssh!' said Noah Bowen, 'the pub is shut'.
> 'Where do you come from?' he said in his buttoned, blue voice. They told him.
> 'I got a auntie there', the policeman said. And very soon he was singing 'Asleep in the Deep'. Off we drove again at last, the charabanc bouncing with tenors and flagons, and came to a river that rushed along among willows.

Since they are never going to reach their destination at the seaside, Porthcawl, they paddle in the 'smooth as a moth's nose' river, and

> dusk came down warm and gentle on thirty wild, wet, pickled, splashing men without a care in the world at the end of the world in the west of Wales. [which is much less childlike] . . . They stopped

at the Hermit's Nest for a rum to keep out the cold. 'I played for Aberavon in 1898', said a stranger to Enoch Davies.

'Liar', said Enoch Davies.

'I can show you photos', said the stranger.

'Forged', said Enoch Davies.

'And I'll show you my cap at home'.

'Stolen'.

'I got friends to prove it', the stranger said in a fury.

'Bribed', said Enoch Davies.

These conversations, and the South Wales emphasis on rugby, beer and hymns, are social history recalled with spirit and accuracy, right down to the policeman's pronunciation of 'a auntie', with hiatus. The child remembers all this with good humour; his day wasn't perfect, he had to amuse himself most of the time (even to throwing a stone at some cows), but this sense of being an observer of the foibles of men, and this tolerance maturing to compassion, would one day inform the poetical prose of *Under Milk Wood*.

19 The Present State of English Grammar

What I have narrated, up to this point, of the history of our grammar is a story of erosion, of 'making do' with fewer forms. The loss of grammatical gender in nouns, and of the declined adjective, is no loss, but a matter for congratulation; but the loss of a dative 'to/for' case for nouns may now seem to readers a pity, the almost total victory of -*s* plural nouns and -*s* singular verbs (over -*n* and -*th*) has certainly impaired the music of the language, the blurred verbs of the 'I set/I set/I have set' type are hardly worth having, and the lack of grammatical agreement between words – where a word can obviously and only have a certain function in the sentence – has meant that dangling phrases (made even more slovenly by the omission of the relative *that*) abound: 'I met the man in the black coat I saw in the market' (the man or the coat?). Are we therefore still shedding the few inflexions which we have? Having lost the subtlety of the subjunctive, shall we go on to make every irregular vowel-changing verb regular by conjugating it with -*d* in the past? There are, in fact, signs that we are still willing to inflect, and *gamesmanship*, *lifemanship* and *oneupmanship* had a vogue: a rather unhappy growth is that of -*wise* attached to a noun for adverbial force: 'He's no good finance-wise', and despite all the fine Old English compound nouns that we have lost, we are still willing to retain, and perhaps extend, verb–noun compound nouns like a 'tell-tale' for checking shifts in engineering or building materials. Ignorant speakers extend the range of -*s*, with 'I knows', 'I goes' and even 'you goes'.

Even when our children, and their elderly imitators, are not using gangster-talk, English tries to get along on too few words. At Gresham's School, Holt, in Norfolk, they have a salutary story of the Victorian headmaster who stepped into the corridor, stopped a boy, and said 'Have the bell rung!' The lad, assuming (a) that it was a question and (b) that whatever the headmaster said was grammatically correct, answered 'No, Sir, it haven't'. In Middle English, the command would have been 'Do/Let ring the bell' or 'Do/Let the bell ring', but now *have* has taken over so many functions that there is further blurring. Yet we seem anxious to adopt pidgin expressions of the no-grammar type, like 'Princess Diana went walk-about' (I suppose it could be argued that this is the only exact way to express it); and we are willing to accept a baffling old 'accusative of reference', clipped and minimal, like 'It's not *that* important'.

I think this over-indulgence in simplicity is a fault, and not to be imitated. But of course, it is not only blurred grammar that makes our writing ambiguous; grammar is not to blame for nasty idioms like 'It won't notice' – the perpetrator here isn't mistaking active for passive, but is just ignorant of what *notice* means. Nor is it grammar's fault that even quite long, clear words develop divergent meanings: the comedian's dialogue, (A) 'I appeal to you!', (B) 'You wouldn't appeal to *anyone*!', depends on what I think is a disastrous happening – with easily the biggest vocabulary in the world, English should be able to manage 'one word, one meaning', but poets might regret this as much as philosophers would welcome it.

At one end of our spectrum of speakers we have those in torpid ignorance, like demagogues on the television who say 'The thing is *is*'; this defies parsing. Worse than they, really, was a recent educationalist who told his trainees that the 'kids' should be allowed to write as they spoke – anything else was 'poncing up the language'. Yet adhering to *our* grammar is no great hardship; remember that our *inflexional* system (not expression eked out by the prepositions *of* and *to*, etc., and the grey verbs *be*, *have*, *do*, *may*, etc.,) has by the present day reduced itself to the following forms, whose reduction we have witnessed down the centuries:

Nouns

The 'normal' s-plural declension:
Nominative (subject of sentence), vocative
(what is called on or addressed), accusative
(object of the verb) singular: it also   *bird, lass*
masquerades as the dative (indirect
object of the verb; the case prefixed
by the 'to/for' idea, as with 'Give the
bird the crumbs').

Genitive (possessive) singular, also	
expressible as 'of the bird'	*bird's, lass's*
Nominative etc. plural	*birds, lasses*
Genitive plural	*birds', lasses'*

(Most nouns in -*y*, and many in -*f*/*fe*,
form their plurals in -*ies* and -*ves*)

The n-plural declension:

Nominative etc. singular	*ox*
Genitive singular	*ox's*
Nominative etc. plural	*oxen*
Genitive etc. plural	*oxen's*

The vowel-changing declension:

Nominative etc. singular	*mouse*
Genitive singular	*mouse's*
Nominative etc. plural	*mice*
Genitive plural	*mice's*

The unchanged-plural declension:

Nominative etc. singular and plural	*sheep*
Genitive singular and plural	*sheep's*

Articles

Definite, undeclined, singular and plural	*the*
Indefinite, undeclined, singular, with -*n* added before vowel or silent *h*-	*a, an*

(no plural; 'some' often used)

And before comparatives, as we have seen, *the* is from an Old English instrumental case, and means 'by so much', as in *The sooner the better*.

Demonstratives (which are adjectives)

'The one over here':   *this*,   plural   *these*
'The one over there':   *that*,   plural   *those*
(I have assumed throughout that my readers are not liable to say 'them things'; but if you *are*, reflect that it is a universal sign of ignorance or vulgarity). Other demonstratives, such as *yon* (der), *same* and *such*, are not declined.

Adjectives

are not declined in any way in the positive – in number, case, gender (save for *this* and *that*).

In the comparative, all adjectives of three of more syllables, and all that end in a suffix, should be expressed by a preceding *more*, and in the superlative by a preceding *most*.

Shorter adjectives, and all the regular ones with one syllable, are compared by means of -(e)r and -(e)st. A few oddities survive, setting no rule for others to fall in with; an Old English superlative -*ma* (like Latin 'primus'), has been given the -*est* suffix additionally, and then this has been muddled with *most*, resulting in *foremost*, *hindmost*, *inmost*, *midmost*, and *utmost* (but *not* creating comparatives like *utmore*). So these are doubled, really, as are the comparatives *lesser* and *nearer*.

But the only difficulty in the comparison of adjectives is, first, in those that change their stems: *old* sometimes *elder*, *eldest*, but regular too; *late*, *lat(t)er*, *la(te)st*; and the antique *nigh*, *near*, *next*, now wrenched right around as *near* and the regular *nearer*, *nearest*. The other irregular adjectives have quite different stems in their second two forms; this obviously applies to *good* and to *bad*, but we tend to forget that *little* is the positive form of *less* and *least*, and *much* of *more* and *most* – *small* and *big* have occupied our minds instead.

I should like to make at this point a personal but not eccentric digression. I have been criticised for saying and writing 'less people', and triumphantly assured that it should be 'fewer people', to which I reply that (a) *few* is an Old English word, but *fewer* isn't, and (b) since 'more milk' and 'more apples' are parallel and correct, so are 'less milk' and 'less apples'.

Adverbs

The word which, as we used to chant as children, 'answers the questions *when*, *where*, *whither*, *whence*, *how* and *why*?' is an adverb; its origins, as the case of a noun – accusative (*somewhat* and – ugh! – *no way*), genitive ('I must *needs*'), dative (*whilom*, a plural), and even locative (*here*, *there*) –, are fascinating, but are hardly our concern now. Effectively, they add -*ly* to the corresponding adjective (*nicely*), or they don't (*fast*); and a lot of wasted anger is generated over whether *loud* (as in Wordsworth's *Poor Susan*) can be used as one.

Conjunctions, Prepositions and Interjections

like *Oh*! may sometimes be broken forms of other parts of speech, but they are now no longer subject to inflection; and, indeed, prepositions work actively against it, modifying the noun beforehand without any help from within it.

Pronouns

It is unnecessary, and far too space-consuming, to set out the paradigm of the pronouns, which stand 'for nouns'. They are easily the most persistent of our ancient grammatical forms, and if we include the second person singular *th-* forms of reverent Christian worship, they remain a rich old paradigm. *I*, *me*, *mine*, *me* cover a host of relationships, and the only regrettable casualty is the *ye* of the 2nd person plural nominative and vocative, which has been levelled to *you* except in the Authorized Version and Common Prayer; pronouns, in fact, have been actually enriched over the years, because the genitive of *it* was once *his* or *hit* or *it* ('It had it head bit off by it young', says Lear's Fool), and the new form *its* was not in fully accepted use until about Dryden's time.

The interrogative pronouns (*who*, *whom*, *whose*, *whom*; *what*, *what*, *of what/which*, *what*?) are still in good order, and the relative pronouns have been borrowed from them. Middle English had normally only the relative *that* (which we can still use, or even omit), but sometimes used *which* – now considered only neuter – as in 'Our Father which art in Heaven'. We are sensitive about using the 'correct' *whom* as an accusative, the object of a verb, but in fact it is quite 'wrong' and is a re-use of the dative. That student dialogue which I mentioned, (a) 'Janet was there' – (b) 'Janet whom?', suggests that *whom* is considered a permanently swankier form than *who*, whatever its function; and 'a man whom I think is coming' is a regular error. Cured of saying, in answer to 'Who's there?', 'Me', we assume that 'I' is altogether preferable, and we universally say 'between you and I'.

Verbs

The verb is of course the most complicated and (not very) richly inflected of our parts of speech. During the course of this book we have seen it in its prime, and then losing most of its foliage and even some of its branches; and it would be repetitious to display it again. Ignoring the 2nd person singular forms, as not in current use save in ripe old rustic speech and in Bristol forms, like *thee bist*, a regular 'weak' verb will now have only the following forms:

Present Indicative: *I/you/we/they kick, he/she/it kicks*.
Present Subjunctive: *he/she/it kick* (well, it's there if you want it).
Past Indicative: *I/you/he/she/it/we/they kicked*.
Past Participle: *kicked*.
Infinitive: *to kick*.
Imperative: *kick*.
Present Participle: *kicking*.
Verbal Noun: *kicking*.

This is a total of four different forms; every other *tense* (the time-sequence of future, perfect, pluperfect, future perfect, and others), *mood* (deviations from statement; wish, doubt, hypothesis), *voice* (the passive, as in 'I am kicked'), *aspect* (especially the continuous tense, for anything that 'is/was happening' when some single things 'happened'), must be expressed by one or more of a wide range of 'auxiliary' verbs – *do, did, has, have, had, will, would, may, might*, etc. There is of course no need to tabulate these; we use them instinctively. But use them with care; they are intrinsically ugly – 'I didn't do it', 'I mightn't've done it' – even though not incorrect, but one nasty new idiom is a parasite in our speech, and deserves to be exposed in an isolated line:

'If I'd've known, I wouldn't've gone'.

The second bit is all right, the first is illiterate for 'If I'd known' or 'Had I known', that nice old quirk of syntax whereby we reverse subject and verb and thus make an *if*-clause.

The irregular 'strong' verbs are as helplessly dependent on the little auxiliaries as are the 'weak' ones, but if we take an exceptionally well-endowed one it will offer us six different forms:

Present Indicative: *I/you/we/they drink, he/she/it drinks*.
Present Subjunctive: *he/she/it drink*.
Past Indicative: *I/you/he/she/it/we/they drank*.
Past Participle: *drunk*.
Past Participle (Passive) – a luxury found in a few verbs: *drunken*.
Imperative: *drink*.

Present Participle: *drinking*.

Verbal Noun: *drinking*.

You may think that 'levelling' the past tense and past participle to *one* form, as in *we sung*, *we have sung*, doesn't matter much. But don't open the floodgates – *I seen him* and *what I done* still matter very much indeed.

This, then, is the shape of our present inflexional system, our grammar, our words as individuals. On this compulsory framework our far more ramified syntax, our constructions, our words as neighbours, can stretch endlessly.

20 The Present State of English Syntax

The old school exercise of analysis and parsing, long abandoned in many schools now, perhaps went about things in the wrong order: you were faced with a passage or sentence of good prose or verse, and you divided it into its component parts and thus showed that it was correctly constructed, which your common sense and your ear should have shown you, anyway. Of course, in the process your good taste should have noticed that it was *well* composed, a model of how to compose, with – say – suspense, balance, inexorable logic, the right words in the right order. But there should have been more analysis of the pupils' careful compositions – revealing, perhaps, a degree of imbalance, disordered items, dangling phrases that formally could belong to either of two nouns or two verbs, and a failure of logic.

Both composition *and* appreciation can begin for a child with 'The cat sat on the mat' (article, noun, verb, preposition, article, noun); it is only a little harder to appreciate fully 'The fat (adjective) cat sat comfortably (adverb) on the black (adjective) mat'; and very soon the group of words hanging together without (phrase) or with (clause) a finite verb could be understood as doing the job of a noun, adjective, or adverb: The fat cat belonging-to-Auntie (adjective phrase), which-had-pale-blue-eyes (adjective clause), lay comfortably with-the-hint-of-a-purr (adverb phrase), when-it-had-finished-its-fish (adverb clause), and occupied what-was-reckoned-a-priceless-oriental-rug (noun clause)'. This sentence (it is meant to be illustrative, not beautiful!) has some faults of weighting, but can serve to show how from the easy yoke of our grammar may hang in bright array streamers of clause and phrase, distinct or interwoven, with no necessity for their being tied in knots.

The 'style' that one may eventually make one's own will emerge

148

from practice and the study of acknowledged masters – imitable ones: it is unlikely that you will become another James Joyce, so do not covet the means to say things like his summing-up of Shem in *Finnegans Wake*:

> O! the lowness of him was beneath all up to that
>   sunk to!

On the other hand, being imitable is no bar to genius; the poet who calls himself (I really don't know why) e.e. cummings must not repel us by this mere typographical trick, especially when we see the traditional beauty of lines in his love-sonnet *it may not always be so*: . . .

> you of my heart, send me a litle word . . .
> Then shall i turn my face, and hear one bird
> sing terribly afar in the lost lands.

I suppose every readable style could be used as a model, but this would always involve a trust in the author's stance. S. L. Bethell, in *The Literary Outlook* (London: Sheldon and New York: Macmillan, 1943), p. 56, coolly pointed out the satisfactory prose of D. H. Lawrence in contrast with the unsatisfactory philosophy: 'No one with a sense of humour could take up the Lawrentian position, which . . . has a good deal in common with the Nazi return to "blood and soil" . . . [Despite recalling us to a sense of 'the profundity of nature' and rescuing sex from the scientists to give it another dimension, he had a] militant attitude; for he preached unreason with the weapons of reason. His prose is logical enough, and will parse and analyse almost as if it had been written from the brain and not the solar plexus. Others, who escaped the mantle of prophecy, were more consistent'.

I hope my readers are all literate, even though many may not understand the mechanics of what they quite elegantly write and speak; but a high degree of literacy may be accompanied by four features of style which are inimical to clear and honest expression: the abstract, the nouny, the passive, and the negative (whose antidotes are the concrete, the verby, the active, and the positive). I devoted a short but meaty chapter to these four nervous symptoms in *The Plight of English* (Newton Abbot: David & Charles, 1975), with the admission that – somewhat rarely – they had their own part to play. Thus the start of Louis XVI's reign in Carlyle's *French Revolution* contains only the verb *to be* and the verbs *resign* and *march*, both as metaphors; yet it vividly conveys the sense that events are germinating and will surely happen:

> There is a stillness, not of unobstructed growth, but of passive inertness, the symptom of imminent downfall. As victory is silent, so is defeat. Of the opposing forces the weaker has resigned itself; the stronger marches on, noiseless now, but rapid, inevitable: the fall and overturn will not be noiseless.

This fine abstraction and nouniness, combined with the chime of verbal nouns in *-ing* and with a string of negative statements, empties of all hope and sense the 1916 trenchscape in the *In Parenthesis* of DAVID JONES (1895–1974), published nearly twenty years after the First World War but still immediate with it. In this passage, a comrade has been killed; despite the arrangement of the lines, I feel the power of this to be as prose, and the barking NCO of the first two lines is a realist, not a mythical brute:

> And get back to that digging can't yer – this aint a bloody Wake
>   for these dead, who will soon have their dead for burial clods
> heaped over
> Nor time for halsing [which with a wonderful play on words is both
> 'embracing' and 'calling on the Divine']
> nor to clip green wounds
> nor weeping Maries bringing anointments
> neither any word spoken
> nor no decent nor appropriate sowing of this seed
> nor remembrance of the harvesting
> of the renascent cycle
> and return
> nor shaving of the head nor ritual incising for these
>   *viriles* under each tree.
> No one sings: Lully lully
> for the mate whose blood runs down.

So the abstract, the nouny and the negative can have their deadly power, as if their subjects were drained; an excess of passives is often much less enjoyable, because false – as if the doer of the action has never existed: I quoted in *The Plight of English* a school's request to me for a reference, in which they just wouldn't use an active verb, and even the covering letter said 'an early reply will be much appreciated'.

This sounds like evasiveness rather than just reticence. Similarly, a flurry of multiple negatives can be very bad style, and in conversation very bad form; I recall the lofty academic who used to corner us with questions like 'Don't you think there's some doubt about the impracticability of abolishing the rule that forbids you to read English if you haven't "O" level Latin unless you're of mature age, but not rescinding the rule of not reading English without it at "A" level . . .?' How would you answer *that* one?

We put many of our negative phrases wrongly. 'I don't think that's very polite' is really intended to be 'I think that's not polite'; we are not interested in a denial of the thought-process. But for years I have stood out mainly against three 'idioms', and incurred the name of pedant for my pains: the improper *if*, the improper *while*, and the improper *(was) to*. Some others, like *literally* in 'I was literally glued to the television', and the misplaced *only* in 'He only died yesterday' are so obviously stupid that I should not have to mention them in a book as decent and serious as this; others, like the split infinitive (unless the split be a gulf) and the actually correct *less people* for 'few people' simply do not matter. But those three objects of my distaste must be tamed and silenced.

If has a big burden already; why do people add to this with remarks like 'There's some jelly in the pantry if you want it' (reasonable answer: 'There's some jelly in the pantry even if I *don't* want it')? Where is the subtlety of 'If the Elgin Marbles leave a gap on the Parthenon, they might have disintegrated up there by now anyway'? – the truth of the first part in no way effects the truth of the second. A third variety, and the silliest, is in a statement I read once that Byron's relationship with his half-sister Augusta, 'if unnatural, was genuine and lasting' – but if demonstrably natural, was ungenuine and fickle? This is fancy style, and no imitator should suppose that it has any merit.

While shows concurrence of events, and means *during the time that, so long as* (I hope, of course, that Northern speakers will continue to use it for 'till' – and *till* for 'to' if they want to). The public now assume that it is a superior way of saying, and especially of writing, *and / but / whereas / though /*; *whilst* is held to be an even more elegant form. Let the well-known old news-item speak for this absurdity: 'The Bishop preached the sermon while the Dean read the lesson'.

I have kept the worst to the last. When something *was to* happen, the clear and only meaning is that it was meant / intended / bound / arranged / ordered / ordained / obliged / predestined to happen. What possible sense can it have in the statement that *Little Dorrit* 'was to be completed in 1858' – there was no such time-limit; this future-in-the-past should be a simple past tense, but it has an offshoot, too – *to* plus an infinitive as if purpose were intended, when it couldn't be. 'Rovers scored a goal in the first half-minute, only to have it disallowed' (deucish sporting of them); *only*, in fact, is normally the fatuous garnish for this phrasing: 'The driver . . . looked out of his window only to be grabbed by the hair' (serve him right). Finally, a little masterpiece from a student essay: 'Troilus sallies out to battle again, to be unexpectedly killed by Achilles' (how do you fix it for the unexpected to occur?).

Needless to say, I might have found examples of these infelicities in the nodding moments of significant or even great authors; to *look* for them would have been indecent and barren, but whoever uses them, they remain bad, and I present them lavishly for your avoidance.

Seem is a misused word which 'seems to be getting commoner'. What does this mean? Something, I suppose like 'I think it is getting commoner, but I'm not prepared to assert this'. If it is thus tentative, I can allow it; but what about 'No one seems to have died of diphtheria there for fifty years'? This is more sinister: they *have* died of it, but it hasn't been diagnosed, so the seeming is fallacious? And they didn't *seem to* die of diptheria when it raged – it was downright and cruelly fatal. What about 'Doctor, I don't/can't seem to be able to concentrate'? Why the subterfuge? – isn't it deceitful to seem to be concentrating? You are able *really*, but seeming to be is the hard part, perhaps. . . Remember always that 'seems to be' hints at 'seems to be, but isn't': 'They seem to be happy together' casts a gloom over the proceedings.

Check every sentence lest you have put a word or phrase in a doubtful relationship with the rest; for ambiguity is the chief fault to avoid, and mere cacophony must not matter by comparison with it. 'I've been trying to 'phone you without success'; well, what a silly and defeatist thing to do! – whereas if you'd been trying without success to 'phone me, no blame would attach to you. 'A 17-year-old child's nanny' has got herself a very strange job; Americans would say *gotten*, which I greatly prefer to *got* for euphony.

Not . . . nor (it should be *not . . . or*, or *neither . . . nor*) goes on being wrong, but in nearly forty years' teaching I have persuaded hardly anyone of this fact. Split infinitives are neither misleading nor always ugly, but I suppose we might as well keep to the 'rule', so often broken by the incomparable Jane Austen. Postfixed prepositions – unless they are brainstorms of them like 'What do you want to pick on a book like *this* to be read to from out of with for?' – are harmless, and much prettier than Sir Winston Churchill's fierce parody 'up with which I will not put'. Loose prepositions, adverbs and conjunctions hurtled together belong to low and unconsidered speech, like 'seeing as how' (it will sound like *seein as ow*). Tattered and desultory sentences plugged with unrelated fragments in this way are proof of indecision and of a breakdown in logic. But don't sneer at *meself*: *myself* contains a possessive, but *himself* doesn't, yet *hisself* is 'wrong'.

Finally, with the evaporation of so much of our old grammatical system, let me emphasise that relationships of words *must* be made clear by careful placing; this can be supported by our very easy system of punctuation. I have not mentioned punctuation deliberately anywhere, because I feel little sympathy for those who say it's difficult (or who write 'I like *it's* texture' about something); but a very good rule is that an adjective clause which defines is not preceded by a comma, but one which describes *is*:

> My son who is a student (I have other sons, but
>   I am here defining the student one);
> My wife, whom I met at Bognor (I have only one
>   wife, of course, and I am describing one facet
>   of her).

Now if anyone writes to you 'My wife whom I met at Bognor', write back and ask how many other spouses he has, and where they met; 'My son, who is a student' suggests that he is an *'only* son'. A language like ours needs its excellent punctuation, but even this prop to undisciplined words cannot achieve everything. That hypothetical husband, if he introduced 'my Greek wife', deserves to be asked, again, how many other spouses he has, and of what nationalities; the only solution here is a complete opening-out of the phrase into something like 'my wife, (*comma*!) who is Greek'.

And there is no solution at all to that lovely exposure of our rickety grammar, the joke which I first heard as:

MAN READING NEWSPAPER: It says here that a man is run over every day in Glasgow.
WIFE: Nonsense! He couldn't stand it.

Index of Authors, Other Persons, Works and Main Grammatical Subjects

OE = Old English; ME = Middle English

155